OPENING THE CLEAR VISION OF THE Mind Only School

by

Khenchen Palden Sherab Rinpoche

and

Khenpo Tsewang Dongyal Rinpoche

Opening the Clear Vision of the

Mind Only School

by

Khenchen Palden Sherab Rinpoche

and

Khenpo Tsewang Dongyal Rinpoche

Edited by Philippe Turenne *and* Pema Dragpa

Opening the Clear Vision of the Mind Only School

Revised Second Edition © 2007 Khenchen Palden Sherab Rinpoche and Khenpo Tsewang Dongyal Rinpoche

First Edition published as *A Glimpse of the Doctrine of the Mind Only School* © 2005 by Dharma Samudra

All rights reserved. No part of this material may be reproduced in any form or by any means, electronic or mechanical, including photocopying, recording, or by any information storage and retrieval system, without prior written permission from the authors.

Published by Dharma Samudra.

Padma Samye Ling
618 Buddha Highway
Sidney Center, NY 13839
(607) 865-8068
www.padmasambhava.org

ISBN: 0-9659339-5-4

Table of Conents

Acknowledgements 9
Preface 11

Introduction 13
- Teachings of the Hinayana and Mahayana 13
- Seven Reasons Why Mahayana is the Great Vehicle 15
  - 1. Great Joyful Effort 15
  - 2. Great Focus 16
  - 3. Great Completion 16
  - 4. Great Wisdom 16
  - 5. Great Skillful Means 17
  - 6. Great Fulfillment 17
  - 7. Great Activity 18
- The Mind Only School 19
  - The Brief Life Story of Vasubandhu 19
  - The Prakaranas of Vasubandhu 25
  - Principal Views of the Mind Only School 28
  - Three Categories of the Mind Only School 28
  - Habitual Patterns 29
  - The Alaya 30
  - The Eight Consciousnesses 31
- Questions and Answers #1 35

The Twenty Verses 45
- Title of the Teaching 46
- Homage of the Translators 46
- The Main Teaching 48
- Establishing the Principal Point: All Phenomena are Only Mind 48
- Establishing the Principal Point by Reasoning 49
  - *Stating the Objection* 49
  - *Refuting the Objection* 50

1. The Dream Example 51
2. The Example of the Hungry Ghost 52
3. Being Harmed in a Dream 53
4. Animals in the Higher and Lower realms 54
5. All Appearances are Only One's Own Perceptions 55
6. Perceptions Arise from the Power of Habitual Tendencies 56
The Importance of this Teaching 60
Questions and Answers #2 63
Establishing Pervasive Certainty 68
Establishing Pervasive Certainty by Scripture 68
The Ayatanas of External Objects Exist 68
The Outer and Inner Ayatanas 70
How to Easily Discover the Two Egolessnesses 71
Self-ego 72
Ego of Phenomena 72
Imputed Phenomena 73
Dependent Phenomena 73
The Fully Established Nature 74

Tibetan Buddhist Logic *77*
The Subject of an Argument 77
Pervasive Certainty 78
Counter-pervasive Certainty 78
Valid and Invalid Cognition 80
Direct Valid Cognition 80
Direct Valid Cognition of the Senses 81
Direct Valid Cognition of the Mind 81
Direct Valid Cognition of Self-Awareness 81
Direct Valid Cognition of Meditators 81
Inferential Valid Cognition 83
Scriptural Valid Cognition 84
Establishing Pervasive Certainty by Reasoning 85
Unitary or multiple atoms cannot be combined 86

Questions and Answers #3 88
The Conjunction of Atoms is Unreasonable 97
The Impossibility of Casting a Shadow or Not 99
The Impossibility of Movement, Place or Size 100
Refuting Objections to the Establishment of Pervasive Certainty by Reasoning 101
The First Refutation 102
The Second Refutation 104
The Third Refutation 106
The Fourth Refutation 107
Questions and Answers #4 109
The Fourth Refutation Continued 115
The Fifth Refutation 116
The Sixth Refutation 121

The Benefits of the Teaching of the Mind Only School 123

Conclusion 127
Mipham Rinpoche's Commentary 127
Longchenpa's Wish-Fulfilling Treasure 127
Questions and Answers #5 130

Summary 139
Imputed Phenomena 139
Exaggeration Without Characteristics 140
Dependently Nominated Entities 140
Dependent Phenomena 141
Impure Dependent Phenomena 141
Pure Dependent Phenomena 142
The Truly Established Nature 142

Meditation Instructions 145
Dedication 149
About the Authors 151
Other Publications by the Authors 157

Acknowledgements

The Samye Translation Group would like to thank everyone who was involved in helping bring this project to fruition. In particular, we would like to thank Philippe Turenne and Pema Dragpa for their joyful effort in completing this book and editing these transcriptions—the second book of this series of shedra teachings—along with their daily activities in support of Padma Samye Ling. Without their aspirations, this book could not have been completed in such a short period of time. We would also like to thank the many people who helped transcribe these teachings, including Andrew Cook, Caroline DiSimone, Mary Ann Doychak, Keith Endo, Elizabeth Guyton, Nancy Lichtenstein, Dimitri Polansky, Esther Sullivan, and Hector Urrutia. Thanks also to Rita Frizzell for her assistance in preparing the text and cover for publishing, and to Sujata Ghosh for her help with the final editing of the text.

We would also like to thank all the resident staff of Padma Samye Ling, including Jomo Lorraine O'Rourke, Pema Tsultrim, Nancy Roberts, Carl Stuendel, Jane Hinson, Celia Barnes, Kate Muller, and Andy Millar, as well as those who have helped with the administration and maintenance of the Padma Samye Ling retreat centers around the world. Without their continuous and unending work, these many projects could not have been fulfilled in such a beautiful way. We also wish to extend our thanks to all members of the Padmasambhava Buddhist Center worldwide for their constant support over many years.

Most importantly, we would like to thank the exceptionally Venerable Khenpo Rinpoches for offering us these medicinal teachings that serve to alleviate the mistaken views distancing us from the true nature that is already and has always been present.

The Venerable Rinpoches wish to offer these deeds as a commemoration of the ancient great masters of these lineages, as well as all practitioners and dharma patrons of the past; in particular, to H.H. Dudjom Rinpoche, their beloved father Lama Chimed Namgyal and their mother Pema Lhadze. They wish to dedicate this merit to the great dharma patrons of our projects, especially Pema Drime and all the others who have passed away. May this volume contribute to creating harmony, peace and happiness now and in the future.

We sincerely ask forgiveness from all wisdom beings, holders of the teachings and readers for all errors and misinterpretations of the teachings present in this text. May all the virtue accumulated through all possible connections with these teachings serve to immediately free all beings from the endless variety of sufferings caused by the narrow, illusory restrictions of dualistic consciousness.

Preface

During the summer of 2003 and 2004 at Palden Padma Samye Ling, the Venerable Khenchen Palden Sherab Rinpoche and his brother the Venerable Khenpo Tsewang Dongyal Rinpoche gave teachings on the Vaibhashika, Sautrantika and Mind Only schools of Tibetan Buddhism. They offered these teachings in accordance with the teaching of Lord Buddha. What is the teaching of the Buddha? It is love and compassion, kindness, non-violence and the realization of selflessness.

Traditionally, the Buddha's teaching is practiced through study and practice. First, one listens to the teachings. Then, one practices with confidence and devotion while reflecting on the meaning of the teachings until it becomes clear in one's mind. One does this by intellectually and systematically investigating the truth of teachings using reason and logic, and by referring to Buddhist scriptures. However, intellectual understanding is not enough to achieve complete realization of the nature of reality. After developing some degree of certainty and understanding concerning the validity and meaning of the teachings, one must then implement this understanding in one's life by practicing and living according to this understanding. This is called meditation.

Over the years at Padma Samye Ling and throughout the various Padmasambhava Buddhist Centers, we have spent a significant amount of time practicing the teachings of Buddhism. Over the past two years, the venerable Rinpoches offered two intensive retreats which focused primarily on studying the very root from which all practice and realization develops. In Tibetan, such intensive study retreats are called shedra. These shedra offer students a valuable opportunity to deepen their knowledge of the different philosophies from which the many different levels of Buddhist practice are derived.

In particular, these two shedra focused on the Vaibhashika and

Sautrantika schools of the Hinayana, and the Mind Only school of the Mahayana. Many great masters of the past and present have correctly understood that the profundity of these teachings is as vast and as deep as the ocean. Through the study and application of these teachings, may the understanding of the Buddha's sublime doctrine swiftly ripen within the hearts and minds of all sentient beings.

Introduction

Generally, according to the Buddha's teaching, the three activities a practitioner should engage in are study, contemplation, and practice. These three are very essential. This is how the Buddha's teachings have continued on until now. Among these three categories, we are mainly focusing on study and contemplation. Of course, we will also focus on the practice of meditation.

To begin any of this, the necessary foundation is to generate a good heart. In the Buddha's teaching this is known as bodhichitta. We then combine this good heartedness with joy and appreciation. This is very important. Cultivating joy and appreciation along with bodhichitta, one should think that, "In order to dispel the darkness of ignorance within myself and in every other living being, I am going to explore the teachings of the Buddha, which is the nature of the truth and the nature of existence and phenomena.

Even though this particular shedra focuses on studying and contemplation, in the Nyingma school the great masters always said not to separate study and contemplation from meditation. When you begin to study the Mind Only school of the Mahayana, reflect on these teachings within the heart and mind, and while you meditate and practice. This is very important, for the purpose of study is to practice. Therefore, please try to combine your studies you're your individual practice. This is an essential point that we need to remember during these shedra programs.

Teachings of the Hinayana and Mahayana

The Buddha, a gracious, kind, and compassionate teacher, gave many different teachings. They are often referred to as the 84,000 different teachings of the Buddha. All of these teachings are summarized into the nine yanas. Even the nine yana teachings can be summarized more simply into two yanas: the Hinayana and Mahayana teachings.

When we look at the history of the Buddhism, the first teaching given by the Buddha was the Hinayana teaching. The Hinayana teaching was very popular during the life of the Buddha because it very much suited with the followers and practitioners of that time. In public, the Buddha gave the Hinayana teachings most of the time. For those who were of high capabilities, the Buddha also gave the Mahayana teaching but he did this very privately and secretly with only those people who were ready to receive these teachings. The Buddha also gave the Vajrayana teachings but they were very secret. There were just not that many people who were ready to receive such profound teachings. Therefore the Buddha's outer, spoken teaching is the Hinayana teaching. The inner teaching is the Mahayana. And the secret teaching is the Vajrayana.

About fifty to one hundred years after Buddha's mahaparinirvana, the Sutra Mahayana teachings began to emerge more publicly due to the circumstances and readiness of the practitioners. So those people who had privately maintained the inner Mahayana teachings shared this with other devoted practitioners and then Mahayana teachings became very popular. Actually, it became more widespread than the Hinayana teachings after about two hundred years following the Buddha's mahaparinirvana.

About three or four hundred years after Buddha's mahaparinirvana the Vajrayana teachings emerged and began to spread more openly and very steadily. These teachings were mainly transferred by the most famous disciples of the Buddha such as Avalokiteshvara, Manjushri and Maitreya, as well as Vajradhara and Vajrasattva. They shared these teachings directly with highly realized beings who then continued to practice them. They also shared the teachings with others, such as those people who came to be known as the eighty-four mahasiddhas. About six or seven hundred years after Buddha's mahaparinirvana many great enlightened beings came one after another. This is just a brief history of how these teachings came about.

Now let us return to the topic of the Hinayana and Mahayana. In Tibetan, Hinayana is known as *thegpa chungngu* and the Mahayana is known as *thegpa chenpo*. Both of these are part of Buddha's teaching. Hinayana has two schools and Mahayana has two primary schools. The Hinayana's two schools are known as the Vaibhashika School and the Sautrantika School. The two schools of Mahayana are known as the Mind Only school and the Madhyamaka School. These are the four doctrinal schools or the four pillars of Buddhism. Every Buddhist teaching falls within the doctrines of these four schools.

Seven Reasons Why Mahayana is the Great Vehicle

Why is the *thegpa chenpo* known as Mahayana or the great vehicle? There are many different explanations of why the Mahayana is a greater vehicle than the Hinayana. The future buddha Maitreya summarizes all of these reasons in his teaching known as the Sutra Alamkara, or *Dode Jen (mdo sde rgyan)*. In this teaching, Maitreya says that there are seven different reasons why Mahayana is the great vehicle. In contrast with the Hinayana, each of these seven qualities is greater or more developed in the Mahayana. The qualities are: 1) great joyful effort (pronounced as *tsondrü chenpo* in Tibetan); 2) great focus or object, which is pronounced *migpa chenpo*; 3) *drubpa chenpo* or great completion; 4) *yeshe chenpo* or great wisdom; 5) great skillful means or *thab khe chenpo*; 6) great fulfillment or *trubpa chenpo*; 7) *tinley chenpo* or great activity.

1. Great Joyful Effort

Let us investigate the meaning of these seven qualities. The first is joyful effort. Compared with the Hinayana, Mahayana practitioners have great joyful effort which lasts for three countless eons. They have great courage, commitment and joy to strive for the goal without becoming tired and bored by the many different circumstances and challenges that they face. They go on and on to fulfill the final goal. Depending on the individual capabilities of the Hinayana practitioners, often it is said that it can take three or seven lifetimes to reach arhathood. Since Hinayana practitioners don't have the long-term goal of continuing to work for the enlightenment of all beings, they don't have to make such long-term plans. This is why the Mahayana practitioners are said to possess great joyful effort.

2. Great Focus

The focus of the Mahayana is also great. The focus of Mahayana practitioners is great emptiness, which includes realizing the emptiness of both self or ego, as well as the emptiness of all phenomena. The Hinayana mainly focuses on realizing the emptiness of self. Mahayana practitioners realize that the nature of all existing phenomena, including the self is great emptiness. Since Hinayana practitioners don't go further than realizing the emptiness of self, the view or focus of Mahayana is said to be greater than that of the Hinayana.

3. Great Completion

The next one is great completion. Mahayana practitioners try to accomplish the benefit of all living beings. In comparison, the Hinayana practitioners mainly think of releasing themselves from suffering by attaining arhathood. Since the Mahayana attempts to reach enlightenment in order to help all living beings, a Mahayana practitioner focuses on other beings' well beings more than his or her own well-being. Therefore, the completion and accomplishment of the Mahayana is greater than that of the Hinayana.

4. Great Wisdom

The great wisdom of the Mahayana includes the wisdom of the egolessness of self and the egolessness of phenomena. This is known as the two wisdoms which realize the egolessness of self and the entire universe without any distinctions. On the other hand, Hinayana practitioners mainly realize the egolessness of the self without fully realizing the egolessness of all other phenomena. In addition, Mahayana wisdom is the union of wisdom and compassion. The wisdom of the Hinayana is without great compassion.

5. Great Skillful Means

The fifth quality is that of skillful means. According to the Mahayana teachings, there are many different skilful means one can apply to remove the obscurations of oneself and others , all in order to accomplish the benefit of all living beings. The skillful means of the Mahayana are based on the Buddha's entire teachings. Mahayana practitioners apply skillful means based on emptiness meditation, as well as on one's own activities. These activities include: rejoicing, dedicating merit, making aspirations, and performing the activities of the six paramitas or perfections, applied continually to all circumstances. There are numerous skillful means. The Mahayana's skillful means are known as the skillful activities that are neither caught in the pain of samsara, nor in the tranquility of nirvana. They go beyond both samsara and nirvana. Hence, in comparison with, the skillful means of the Mahayana are greater than those of the Hinayana.

6. Great Fulfillment

Next is the quality of great fulfillment. By continually practicing and applying oneself according to the Mahayana path, the achievement will be Buddhahood, whereas the attainment of the Hinayana is arhathood. Buddhahood however, is completely free of all defilements and blockages, bondages and every type of habitual pattern. Both arhathood and Buddhahood are free from negative emotions. However, unlike arhathood, when you reach Buddhahood there are no longer any shadows or stains of any type of obscuration that remain in one's consciousness.

7. Great Activity

Once you reach the final goal of Buddhahood, you continually engage with the world in order to benefit all living beings. This happens through the four kayas and the five wisdoms. Reaching Buddhahood is reaching out to every living being without partiality. In contrast, in the Hinayana once you reach arhathood, your activity ceases. According to the Buddha's teaching, there is nothing more than to accomplish or do for the Hinayana practitioner. These are the seven special reasons why the Mahayana is known as the great vehicle.

The Mind Only School

According to the nine yana teachings, the beginning of the Mahayana is known as the Bodhisattvayana. The Bodhisattvayana has two subdivisions: the Mind Only school and the Madhyamaka School. For our teaching this year we are investigating the Mind Only school in particular.

All the great masters of the Mind Only school said that every teaching the Buddha gave was a teaching on the Mind Only school. In general, the history of the Mind Only school officially begins with the great master Vasubandhu. The importance of Vasubandhu was predicted by Buddha Shakyamuni himself. Before Vasubandhu, there were many great masters of the Mind Only School such as Shankarananda. Among these many great masters none became as popular and powerful as Vasubandhu.

The Brief Life Story of Vasubandhu

Soon after Buddha, the great teacher came into this world; India was filled with many great masters and practitioners. The whole country was named the land of Aryas, the Holy Land, because there were so many great beings that truly represented love, kindness, and compassion, free from the ego and selfish thoughts. The whole land was filled with these beings shining as brilliant suns. Many great masters came one after another. Among these great masters, in Buddhist history you often hear of the "Six Ornaments" and the "Two Supreme Ones." Vasubandhu is one of the "Six Ornaments." The great master Vasubandhu wrote many books that reveal the deep meaning of the Buddha's teaching through logic and reason. One of these books is the *Twenty Verses*, which explains that everything is mind.

Vasubandhu was a genius. Initially, he was a great scholar of the

Hinayana. While he was a great Hinayanist scholar he wrote the famous text, the *Abhidharmakosha*. Abhidharma is often translated into English as Buddhist Psychology, but this is not entirely accurate since it deals not only with the mind, but with the entirety of existing phenomena. In a way, the *Abhidharmakosha* is a condensed teaching of the entire Hinayana teaching.

Vasubandhu is one of the great teachers in the history of Buddhism. Buddha Shakyamuni predicted that Vasubandhu would come. He lived during the early times when Buddhism was spreading, existing, and shining in India. At that time, he was named the "Second Buddha." Every school referred to him in this way because his knowledge of different levels of Buddhism was so incredibly vast.

Master Vasubandhu was a great scholar of all of the Buddhist as well as non-Buddhist schools. He studied both the Buddhist schools and non-Buddhist schools, thoroughly examining and analyzing them using both logic and reasoning. It is often said that Vasubandhu is the great master who crossed the oceans of both Buddhist and non-Buddhist schools. He then taught about the experience of what he achieved. The final conclusion that he came to is the teaching of the Mind Only school.

In the life story of Vasubandhu it is said that he memorized the Buddha's entire teaching, ranging from the Hinayana through all of the Mahayana. He memorized all of the different topics of the Buddha's 999,000 teachings. In order to not forget these teachings, every month for fifteen days he recited the teachings non-stop. Because he used so much energy during his recitation, it is said that he sat down in a tank filled with raw mustard seed oil. You could only see him from the neck up. In this way he would chant all of the Buddha's teachings from memory.

During his life he was one of the great masters who gathered many hundreds of thousands of followers. Whenever he traveled on pilgrimage to various holy places, over a thousand students always accompanied him. He was one of the rare masters of that time. Many of the masters during his time lived and stayed in isolated hermitages. Master Vasubandhu, on the other hand, was always accompanied by over a thousand students, and hundreds of thousands of people would gather to receive teachings from him.

Vasubandhu often said that his four foremost students were even more scholarly than himself. The first is Master Lodrö Tenpa (*Blo gros bstan pa*). He was even more of an expert in the Abhidharma than Vasubandhu himself. In Sanskrit this master's name is Chitramati.

The next disciple is Acharya Chokchi Langpo (*phyogs kyi blang po*), which in Sanskrit is Acharya Dignaga. Chokchi Langpo was more expert in logic than Vasubandhu himself.

The third disciple is master Namdrol De. He is more of an expert in the Prajnaparamita than Vasubandhu himself. His name is Vimuktasena in Sanskrit.

And then Master Yonten Ö was more of an expert in the Vinaya than Vasubandhu himself. In Sanskrit his name is Guna Prabha.

These four great masters in particular were honored by Vasubandhu as being even more knowledgeable and scholarly than him in their respective subjects. They are often called the "Four Great Pillars of Vasubandhu's teaching." But there are so many great masters who were disciples of Vasubandhu, and each of these great masters also had many famous disciples. Therefore it is often said that the chain of great scholars in Vasubandhu's lineage of the Mind Only school is like a chain of great lions, or like a chain of golden mountains. These great enlightened beings came one after another, restrengthening the Buddha's teachings at the academic level, as well as the level of realization or achievement.

For example, the famous logician Dharmakirti was a great disciple of Vasubandhu. Dharmakirti was also the grand-disciple of Acharya Dignaga, or Chokchi Langpo. Dignaga and Dharmakirti are two of the most famous logicians in Buddhist history. They are the founders of the Buddhist system of logic.

Great master Shantarakshita was also a great-great-great-disciple of Vasubandhu's. He was connected to Namdrol De, who was more of an expert of the Prajnaparamita than Vasubandhu himself. Shantarakshita also received teachings about logic from one of Dharmakirti's third generation disciples. There are many great masters in Vasubandhu's lineage. Historically speaking, Vasubandhu is one of the greatest masters who spread Buddha's entire teachings.

Mahayana Buddhist history often mentions the "Six Ornaments of the World." This refers to six great Buddhist masters; namely Vasubandhu, Acharya Dignaga, Guna Prabha, Shakya Prabha, Dharmakirti and Aryadeva. Among these six, four of them are connected to Vasubandhu's lineage of the Mind Only school. Of course there is Vasubandhu himself. Two of the others are direct disciples of Vasubandhu—Acharya Dignaga and Guna Prabha. Shakya Prabha is a disciple of Guna Prabha.

Vasubandhu had many teachers. His Hinayana teacher was Lopön Dubzang or Sanghabhadra in Sanskrit. His Mahayana teacher was his elder brother Lopön Tokme or Asanga. According to Buddhist history, Asanga and Vasubandhu were brothers who had the same mother but different fathers. Their mother was named *Prakashashila (Salwe Ngangtsulma, gsal ba'i ngang tshul ma)*. She was a very great enlightened being. It is said that she was a great bodhisattva who was born as a woman in order to restrengthen the teaching of the Buddha. By the power of her aspirations she had two sons from two different fathers. When each of her sons had grown up they asked what their fathers' work was. She told them that she didn't have them both in order to follow their father's profession. She had the intention that they would follow the teaching of their Great Father, the Buddha. As they grew up, she sent them to different places to study Buddhism. She sent her elder son to Nalanda to mainly study the Mahayana. She sent her younger son to Kashmir. At that time Kashmir had large Buddhist schools that specialized in the Hinayana teachings. Later, her sons became known as

Asanga and Vasubandhu.

According to modern history, Asanga and Vasubandhu's birthplace was in Pakistan. When Gendün Chöpel, a great master and scholar of the twentieth century, visited India, he indicated that their birthplace was close to Raulpangi in Pakistan. In ancient times, this area was considered part of India.

Asanga went to Nalanda and studied all of the different Buddhist teachings. Eventually he became a great scholar. However, he still had many questions about the Prajnaparamita teachings. He contacted many great masters and none of them totally clarified his questions. So he asked them who the greatest expert of the Prajnaparamita teachings was. Everybody said that the future buddha Maitreya was an expert in the Prajnaparamita teachings but that they could not see him because he was in a different realm called Tushita Heaven. One cannot see him unless one achieves realization by meditating and practicing on Maitreya. Because of this Asanga received teachings, empowerment and instructions on Maitreya, and then he meditated for about twelve years on Maitreya. This was a long process. Many of you already know this story.

As Asanga studied the Mahayana and eventually became an expert in Mahayana teachings, his younger brother Vasubandhu was studied the Hinayana. During this time Vasubandhu completely adopted the Hinayana position and tried to disprove the Mahayana teachings. Vasubandhu even said to his older brother, "How pathetic! It is so pathetic that you went to the jungle for twelve years, didn't really achieve any realization, and then instead of practicing you wrote enough books to fill an entire elephant load. How pathetic this is."

In a way, Vasubandhu disproved of the Mahayana teachings and so he criticized them. In response, Asanga felt a compassion for his younger brother. He knew the potential of what Vasubandhu could become. The time seemed right to help Vasubandhu, so Asanga asked two of his disciples to take two texts and go to a place nearby where

Vasubandhu was staying. In Tibetan the names of the texts are the *Sapchupa (Sa bcu pa)* and the *Salujampa*. In English these sutras are called the *Sutra of the Ten Bhumis* and the *Green Rice* or *Green Harvest Sutra*. Asanga instructed these two disciples to recite the Green Harvest Sutra in the morning and to recite the Ten Bhumi Sutra in the evening. He wanted Vasubandhu just to hear these sutras. Asanga knew that Vasubandhu was an intelligent person and that once he heard these teachings he would understand what the Mahayana is about. The disciples followed Asanga's instructions. Thus, in the morning they read the Green Harvest Sutra and in the evening they read the *Sutra of the Ten Bhumis*.

When Vasubandhu heard these sutras he immediately knew that the Mahayana was very profound. He recognized that it had a good view, good conduct, and a good result. But since he did not believe in anything blindly, he wanted to debate with Asanga in order to establish his knowledge of the Mahayana through reason and logic.

Asanga and Vasubandhu finally got together to debate points of the Hinayana and Mahayana. The debate lasted quite a long time. With each question and response Vasubandhu was very sharp and smart, direct, and quick. Asanga answered all of Vasubandhu's questions. But rather than answering the questions immediately, Asanga would pause for a short while and then give a very good answer. This happened many times. Finally, Vasubandhu asked his elder brother why he always hesitated before giving him an answer.

Asanga said that he was not like his younger brother. When he asked Maitreya about Vasubandhu, Maitreya said that Vasubandhu had been born as a scholar for five hundred lifetimes. Therefore, Asanga's sharpness and intelligence could not compare with his brother's. He could not debate as well as Vasubandhu. So Asanga would ask the difficult questions to Maitreya and Maitreya would then give him the answers.

By this time Vasubandhu's mind had become very comfortable with the Mahayana teachings. By using logic and reasoning while debating with Asanga he had received enough answers to his questions that he reached a conclusion. He developed the wisdom of certainty that Mahayana was an authentic teaching of the Buddha that was very great. Around the same time that he realized this, Vasubandhu asked Asanga if he could also see Maitreya. Asanga asked Maitreya this question. Maitreya told Asanga that Vasubandhu would not be able to see him during this lifetime. Vasubandhu criticized and disapproved of the Mahayana teachings and because of this he had obscured his relationship with Maitreya.

Then Vasubandhu felt really very bad. He knew that he had made many terrible mistakes. Maitreya told him not to worry or feel sad about this. He asked Vasubandhu to write commentaries on the Mahayana and to practice Mahayana teachings. Because of this he would see Maitreya sooner or later, so he didn't have to feel bad about his previous errors.

Vasubandhu went on many pilgrimages with many of his students. Near the end of his life, he went with his students to visit the place that is now known as Kathmandu, Nepal. In Kathmandu, near Sherenbamath there is a very famous stupa. He passed away very close to this stupa. Even now his relics are in this stupa. Everybody goes there to pay respect. Often it is said that this is the stupa of the great master Vasubandhu.

This is the brief life story of the great master Vasubandhu.

The *Prakaranas* of Vasubandhu

Vasubandhu wrote many books which deal with both the Hinayana schools and the Mind Only school of the Mahayana. Among these, most of his works dealing with the Mind Only school are known as the eight *Prakaranas*. These eight different books deal with the different philosophies the Mind Only school. Of these eight works of

Vasubandhu, the first is known as the *Thirty Verses* or *Thirty Stanzas (Sum Chupa)*. The *Thirty Verses* argues that the entire universe is no other than mind.

The second *Prakaranas* is the *Twenty Verses (Nyi Shupa)*. This teaching was written to support and prove the arguments of the *Thirty Verses* by using logic, reasoning and citations of scriptures from the Buddha's teaching. It uses these to provide evidence which establishes that all existing phenomena are mind.

Vasubandhu's next text is roughly translated as *Description of the Five Aggregates (Phung Nga'i Namzhag Tönpa)*. This teaching explains how the five aggregates can exist if everything is mind. It says that even if everything is mind, phenomena can still function perfectly—the five aggregates can work perfectly. It explains this clearly through logic.

The fourth text is *Establishing that the Activities of the Three Doors are Perfectly Suited (Gosum Thepa Drubpa'i Rabje)*. If everything is mind how can the subject, object and activities of the body, speech and mind function? *Gosum* means the three doors of the body, speech and mind. This text demonstrates that even if everything is mind, the functions and activities of the body, speech and mind are perfectly suited. They are perfectly O.K. He wrote this teaching to explain how this is true according to logic and reasoning.

Clearly Explaining the Systems (Namshe Rigpa) is Vasubandhu's fifth *Prakarana* or treatise. In this teaching, he explains what Dharma is, how teachers should teach students, and how students should receive the teachings. He explains the system and the nature of the teaching, teacher and student very thoroughly and clearly.

These five books are known as the *Five Self-Composed Treatises* of the great master Vasubandhu. Vasubandhu wrote these five books himself. There are three other books he wrote as commentaries on other great masters' teachings about the Mind Only school.

Generally, the story goes that after Vasubandhu's brother Asanga practiced on the future buddha Maitreya for twelve years, Maitreya gave him five different teachings that explained the Buddha's entire teaching. Often these teachings are known as the *Five Teachings of Maitreya* or the *Five Teachings of Asanga*. Vasubandhu wrote commentaries on three of the five texts of his elder brother Asanga which he received from Maitreya. Of these three texts, the first is known as *Utha Namje (dbu mtha' rnam 'byed)*, which is roughly translated into English as *Distinctions of the Middle and Extremes*. This is one of Maitreya and Asanga's teachings. In Sanskrit it is called *Madhyantavibhaga*. The second teaching of Maitreya and Asanga is *Cho Dang Cho Nyid Namje*, which is roughly translated as *Distinguishing Phenomena and the Nature of Phenomena*. In Sanskrit it is called *Dharmadharmatavibhaga*. The third work of Maitreya and Asanga is *Thegpa Chenpo Dojen (Theg pa chen po'i mdo rgyan)* which is roughly translated as *Ornament of the Mahayana Sutras*. In Sanskrit it is called *Mahayanasutralamkara*. Out of the five works of Maitreya and Asanga, Vasubandhu wrote commentaries on the three works listed above. He wrote the commentaries in a way that was directed towards the Mind Only school.

This is a brief history of the Mind Only school. It is good to know about the source of the Mind Only school and how it started. Of course there is more to say about this—this is just very brief history. In the Dzogchen teachings it is said that it is always necessary and important to tell the history and source of a teaching. If you don't know the history of a teaching it will be baseless and you will be in a dilemma. The source of a teaching is told according to a particular lineage. We must always explain teachings according to their particular history.

In this part of our shedra program we are dealing with the Mind Only school. We are going to teach according to the teachings of Longchenpa and Mipham Rinpoche, and then combine them with the *Twenty Verses* of Vasubandhu. We will try to discuss and explain the Mind Only school in this way. Mipham Rinpoche wrote very brief commentaries on the *Nyi Shupa (Twenty Verses)* and I wrote the textual outline giving all the different sections of the text. In Tibetan this is called *sab che (sa bcad)*. We will discuss this teaching according to each of these texts.

Principal Views of the Mind Only School

First, let us look at the principal views of the Mind Only school, or the *Sem tsam pa (sems tsam pa)* in Tibetan. It accepts the alaya (*kun zhi*). This means that everything that we perceive externally is no other than the display of the mind. Non-mental entities do not exist. There is nothing that exists separately or independently from the mind. Everything is mind.

Three Categories of the Mind Only School

The Mind Only school divides everything into three categories. The alaya is the foundation. Besides the alaya, everything is divided into the universe, the five objects of the five senses, and one's own body. According to the Mind Only school, everything is within the three categories of place or universe, objects of the five senses, and one's own body.

So why do we see all of these things? It is because of our habitual patterns. Where do we keep these habits? What is the object that is perceived? This universe is the object; this planet, this mountain and this country, and its waters, rivers and oceans. These are a few obvious examples of external objects which exist.

The second category is what is directly communicated between oneself and the object. This is known as *dön nga* in the Mind Only School. *Don* can be roughly translated as "the objects of the five senses" because they are directly communicated to you. The object of the eye consciousness is form. The object of the ear is sound. Form, sound, smell, taste and touch are all known as *don* —the objects of the senses.

The individual body that is closely connected to oneself is known as the aggregates. The aggregates coalesce according to the conditions of one's karma. Take human beings, for example. Human beings walk with two feet and use two arms. Animals walk by using both their legs and their arms. Birds fly with two legs and use their beaks for almost every purpose. These characteristics depend on the different individual and the species. There are so many different beings, but no matter what the circumstances, physical characteristics are included within the aggregate of form or body.

Habitual Patterns

These are all known as habitual patterns (*bak chak, bag chags*): habit of the object, habit of one's own self and habit of the use of one's own self. Generally speaking, these three habits are based on grasping and clinging. We have the habit of truly existing objects. We have the habit of a truly existing body. We have the habit of the truly existing objects of the senses. Clinging and grasping become convenient and regularly used by us. This is called a habit. You learn a habit and you follow the habit until it becomes very casual. Then, it seems natural to you. But these habit patterns all began with the mind.

How do these habits begin to develop? Habits begin to accumulate and strengthen due to the activities of consciousness. Consciousness first begins using the habit, externally projecting based on a particular habit, and then grasping at the projection as though it truly existed. As this continues, one becomes accustomed to the habitual patterns, which repeatedly imprint themselves on the subtle consciousness of the alaya. The habit gradually becomes stronger and stronger.

Habits are qualified according to the situation and circumstances that one faces. If a circumstance and situation is going smoothly and beautifully in a nice way, this is known as being virtuous. If a circumstance and situation is happening in a very unpleasant way, this is a negative or non-virtuous habit pattern. A circumstance and situation that occurs as a mixture of pleasantness and unpleasantness is known as a mixture of the virtuous and non-virtuous. According to this, the mind experiences itself, based on the circumstance or situation that is arising. This mind then reflects this experience back to itself. We call these instances suffering and happiness, or sadness and sorrow.

All of this happens in the same way in which a dream takes place. There is really no difference between what you are experiencing now and what you experience at night when you dream. While you dream you are not going to think that it is a dream. It seems that the dream is truly happening until we gain some understanding or wisdom. We only recognize that a dream is a dream after we wake up. Otherwise we believe that it's real and it's true.

There are so many varieties of dreams. We can dream about mountains, lakes and horses; men and women; friends and enemies; gaining and losing; beauty and ugliness. So many things can happen in dreams. Everything that we experience while we are awake happens in the dream world. On the reality level, there is really no difference between one's dreams during the night and the dreams of our daytime experience. The moment we wake up, all of the display of a dream disappears. Similarly, when we wake up, dispel the darkness of the ignorance and cleanse our habitual patterns, then our vision and our perception becomes completely different. At that time, our perception or state is known as Buddhahood. Buddhahood is another aspect or dimension of the display of the mind.

The higher Vajrayana teachings often refer to the land of Great Bliss, saying that you are the mandala of the Great Bliss. There is nothing other than the reflections of your own mind and your own display.

The Alaya

Everything is kept in the alaya. Simply speaking, the alaya is nothing other than the mind. But what exactly is the alaya? Alaya is a Sanskrit word. In Tibetan it is *kunzhi. Kun* means "all" and *Zhi* means "foundation or base." So *kunzhi* can be roughly translated as the "ground of all," "base of all," or the "foundation of all." In a way, alaya is consciousness but it is very subtle and balanced. The base of consciousness is very calm, pervasive, and brilliant. It doesn't have partialities. It registers and keeps all of the memories experienced by the mind. It is impermanent; yet, it continues uninterruptedly as the chain of subtle subconscious events. It does not swing back and forth like our thoughts and conceptions. The nature of the alaya is obscured but it has no partialities (*long ma teng*). If somebody asks whether the alaya is virtuous, we cannot say that it is virtuous. We also cannot say that it is non-virtuous. Neither can we say that it is between virtuous and non-virtuous. Therefore, it is said to have no partialities (*long du ma ten pa*). It impartially registers everything that the mind experiences without exception. Yet alaya is also not as bright and clear as mind. In a way, it is very vague but very equal. And since it has no partialities, it is balanced. It encompasses everything without excluding anything.

The Eight Consciousnesses

In a more detailed way, the alaya can be divided into the seed alaya and the maturing alaya. The alaya is the eighth consciousness. It is the source of the seven other consciousnesses. In a way, the seven other consciousnesses are like the retinues of the alaya. The seven consciousnesses are feed the state of the alaya. The first six consciousnesses include eye consciousness, ear consciousness, nose consciousness, tongue consciousness, body consciousness and mind consciousness (*sem*). These are called the six groups of consciousnesses of the six senses. The seventh consciousness is known as the emotion-clinging consciousness. It is the consciousness that mainly projects the sense of self and the importance of this sense of self. Altogether these are known as the seven consciousnesses. These consciousnesses are the arising sparking state of the alaya as is needed or in response to different circumstances and situations. Therefore these seven consciousnesses are often referred to as the tides, waves, and ripples of ocean of alaya. The *kunzhi* or alaya is like an ocean. Although the six consciousnesses change and move in many different ways like the waves, ripples and tides of the ocean, eventually they return to the ocean of alaya.

Whenever we act with the seven consciousnesses operating, every instance and every movement is registered or imprinted in the alaya regardless of whether it is virtuous, non-virtuous or a mixture between the two. For example, when we see beautiful things and we start clinging onto them, this is imprinted or registered in the alaya. If we respond to ugly and unpleasant things with hatred or a sense of rejection, this shadow or imprint is also registered in the alaya. When we experience a regular kind of conception where there is neither hatred nor attachment, this simple, regular thought is also imprinted. Even joy, devotion, positive mental states, and good deeds are imprinted in the alaya according to the intensity with which we perform an action or develop a quality. Whatever is imprinted in the alaya eventually begins to reflect back to you and is experienced through your senses.

Therefore according to the Mind Only School, everything is imprinted on the alaya. Every experience is imprinted on the alaya as a memory or habitual pattern which occurs through the nervous system and the brain and whatever else in the body which may be included. The imprints use these physical systems like a canal or a wire, but are imprinted in the alaya. That's why some people can have memories from far beyond this present life. Our experience occurs according to the different imprints registered in our alaya which are being reflected back to us externally.

For example, if we register more positive, virtuous moments in our alaya then when the six consciousnesses begin sparked due to these imprints, they bring about that same positive, virtuous energy and vision through to the senses. This is how it begins to be reflected externally. As a result, everything appears beautiful and you experience happiness. This can happen if you previously imprinted loving kindness, compassion and joy in the alaya. The imprints are not just going to stay there for awhile and then disappear. Eventually they will be reflected through the senses, appearing as waves of light shining through you. As a result, everything will look really beautiful and really good even if external situations and circumstances appear very terrible. Such individuals are very happy, joyful, and content because their virtuous imprints are being reflected back through their past experiences.

This is why the places in the world where great beings who registered many positive imprints in their alayas and became enlightened are very beautiful. The power of this is not just experienced by these individuals. It can be experienced by other beings as well. Such places become holy spots or places of pilgrimage because of the energy or power that was left by great beings.

Similarly, some people previously registered so many negative, non-virtuous imprints in their alaya that as a result, they constantly stay in fear, worry, sadness, and suffering. This is because what they did earlier was registered in the alaya, which later reflected right back to themselves. This can also be due to the power of negative forces which can also saturate certain places in our surroundings with negative energy. People can become easily frightened or uncomfortable, and unpleasant things can happen in these places. Hence, the shadow or residue of the experience of the alaya can leave behind great darkness.

However, really the alaya is nothing other than the mind. Alaya is mind. In addition to the alaya and the seven other consciousnesses, there are also another five kinds of consciousnesses, or retinues. The first retinue is that of feeling, which is followed by conception, thinking, touching, and rethinking or analysis. Analysis means the chain of thinking which follows an initial thought. Most of the time, our thinking is not just related to what is happening in the present moment. As a thought arises, this leads to another thought, and then another. This continues on for some time. Many thoughts occur based on a single, first thought. This is known as *yi la cho pa* in Tibetan, or rethinking.

All of this is the view of the Mind Only school. In Tibetan, the Mind Only school is called *Sem tsampa*. *Sem* is "mind." *Tsam* means "only."

Pa is a possessive particle; hence, the full term means "one who follows the view of the Mind Only." The Mind Only school is therefore *sem tsampa*. In Sanskrit it is called *Cittamatra*. 'Chitta' is mind. 'Matra' is only, or "Mind Only"

The Mind Only view is a Mahayana teaching. Actually, it is part of the foundation of Mahayana philosophy, which is an essential teaching revealed by the Buddha. From the Mind Only school all the way through go the Vajrayana teachings, and even to the Dzogchen Atiyoga teachings, everything is mind. There are really no big differences amongst all of the philosophical approaches of each school.

Still, people ask followers of the Mind Only school: "What about these mountains and this river? They look so solid and tangibly existing, but the mind is not exactly like that. So why do we perceive things as solidly existing?" The Mind Only school answers that this is only due to our habitual patterns. Because we have developed so many habitual patterns as a result of clinging and grasping, we believe that phenomena truly exist. We have cling and grasped for such a long time, that our experience appear as solidly existing things. Otherwise, everything is complete emptiness, like shadows or the reflections of your mind.

This is briefly the essential teachings and views of the Mind Only school. Everything is mind. Of course, all of this is explained with logic and reasoning. The *Twenty Verses* of Vasubandhu explain all of this, which we will discuss, stanza by stanza. We will also refer to the teachings of Longchenpa and Mipham Rinpoche. This is just a very brief outline of the principal views of the Mind Only school.

Questions and Answers #1

Question: Some Mahayana schools don't subscribe to Vajrayana Buddhism. Could you please speak about this?

Answer: Practitioners of basic Buddhism or the Hinayana don't really agree with many of the Mahayana teachings and philosophy. They definitely do not agree with Vajrayana teachings. Vajrayana teachings are a little too crazy for them, I think.

Some people who practice basic Buddhism say that Buddhism started off fine in Tibet but then it became deluded by Hindu Brahmanism. They think that Vajrayana teachings are a mixture of Buddhism and Hinduism. This is been openly discussed.

There are not many philosophical differences between the Mahayana and Dzogchen. The Hinayana is the foundation teaching and from there Buddhism gradually moves forward. Dzogchen is the ultimate teaching. For this reason the great master Longchenpa said in one of his teachings that when you are in the lower mountains and looking up at the higher mountain ranges, it is difficult to see all the way up. But when you are on the peak of the upper mountains, you can see clearly what is beneath you. From the apex, you see how the top is related to the bottom. Similarly, the schools of the lower yanas or basic Buddhism don't exactly, from their perspective, see how clear and brilliant everything is. But when you look down from the higher yanas you can see how the teachings are connected. You can then understand how the lower teachings are entirely necessary to support wherever you're standing in the Vajrayana teachings.

The Mahayana teachings can be divided into two sections. These are called the sutra Mahayana and tantra Mahayana teachings. The teaching that we are talking about now is from the sutra Mahayana. Among the sutra Mahayana teachings, we are discussing the Mind Only school.

Question: Rinpoches, you mentioned that the Mahayana school consists of the Cittamatra and Madhyamaka. How do the Vajrayana and Dzogchen views incorporate these schools? Is there any particular conflict between the two?

Answer: No, according to the Dzogchen teachings, they don't contradict each other. Even the Hinayana teachings are not going to conflict. It is just a different way of explaining the nature of reality to different beings. In particular, the Mind Only school and Madhyamaka schools are the foundation of Dzogchen. Therefore they are really not going to conflict. In the Dzogchen, everything just becomes even more clear and elaborated. It is a more direct pointing out of these teachings.

Question: Why do some people follow the basic Buddhism teachings, others follow the Mahayana and still even more people do not agree with Buddhism at all?

Answer: One of the teachings in the Mind Only school is on different types of minds. In Tibetan there is the word *rig* (*rigs*), which can be translated as "family, race, caste or gene." In Sanskrit they call it *gotra.* The Mind Only school classifies different types of minds into five different categories or families. These five families are as follows: the shravaka family, the pratyekabuddha family, the bodhisattva family, the uncertain type of family, and then the category of not being part of any particular family. These five families encompass every living being. Their capabilities, mentalities, and personalities all fall within these five categories.

The people who are in the shravaka category are completely going to stick with the Hinayana or shravakayana teaching even when they hear Mahayana teachings or anything other teachings. Even if you pull at them, it won't go into their ears. Instead, it will go from one ear out the other ear. It just passes directly through them. So you cannot change someone who is in this particular family. People of the shravaka family stay within the shravaka family.

The same is true for the pratyekabuddha family. No matter what circumstances or situations you create around someone in this family, whoever has this type of mind is going to strongly resist any type of change from outside of their family type. They will remain within the pratyekabuddha family.

Similarly, those who are in the bodhisattva family are not going to change their habitual tendencies even if they are in the middle of the Hinayana. Their mind is completely different. They are going to have a strong tendency to retain Mahayana qualities and activities regardless of circumstances.

Beings in the uncertain family are neutral. They are not predisposed to anything in particular. Whatever circumstances and situations occur will influence their minds according to that particular direction. So they are not really in a fixed category. If they become connected to the Hinayana, their mind will develop according to the Hinayana and they will follow Hinayana practices. If they are connected with the bodhisattvayana, they will gradually begin to follow the bodhisattvayana. There is no certainty of mind for this type of being. Everything is able to change pretty easily.

Finally there is the category of having no family—the family of no-family. For this type of being, no matter what the situation or circumstance, he or she will not change anything. Things will just stay as they are. There will be no improvement. It will be very difficult for any kind of change to occur. This kind of individual is not going to accept any teachings or any kind of spirituality. They will not be receptive to any kind of deeper meaning. That's it. They're stuck and they will stay that way. These are the five different families of beings.

Question: If someone doesn't have the "gene" for spirituality (i.e., is in the category of no-family) does this continue from lifetime to lifetime? Can anything cause one type of mind to change to another type of mind?

Answer: Yes, even beings in the category of no-family can change from lifetime to lifetime because they have buddha-nature. Therefore, someone who is not very receptive to spiritual teachings can change over time, but it will be very hard and is a long process. Because their mind is so obscured and they do not have many kinds of sparking, shining things within their mind already, it will take a long time to change from the no-family type of mind into a different type of mind like the bodhisattva family.

Question: Could you say a little more about the distinction between skillful means for the Mahayana and the Hinayana?

Answer: The simple way to tell the difference between the skillful means and activities of the Hinayana and Mahayana is by looking at compassion. Compassion is the biggest skillful means of the Mahayana. Of course this compassion is in union with wisdom. The Hinayana definitely also has compassion—all of Buddha's teachings are based on compassion and love. However, the compassion of the Hinayana is a little limited. This is the biggest difference between these two yanas. Because of this difference in compassion, practices such as six paramitas are slightly different. Because of compassion, Mahayana practitioners will wish to accomplish the benefits of every living being. Hinayana practitioners don't really possess such thoughts.

Skillful means are generally associated with relative truth. Compassion is related to relative truth. Because of compassion we, are able to develop bodhichitta. Because of bodhichitta we aspire to help all beings and dedicate our merits for the sake of all beings. All of this is known as skillful means activities.

For example, the compassion of the Mahayana is easily recognized in the aspirations of bodhisattvas. For example, they make the aspiration to take birth in any form that can benefit other beings. No particular form is designated. This includes every possible form that may help other beings. This also includes any range of service that is beneficial. Practitioners of the Hinayana do not make aspirations like this. Mahayana practitioners also make aspirations to take rebirth in any realm wherever their help is needed. According to the Mahayana, you do not wish to remain only in one realm. Bodhisattvas will take any form and go anywhere to help others. It is not exactly the case in the Hinayana teachings. Another aspiration of the bodhisattvas is to complete all the six paramitas, together with performing the deeds that are necessary to carry this intention into action, thinking, "May I also help mature all living beings until they reach buddhahood, and may I have the ability to transform this universe into a pure land and free every living being from all types of suffering." These aspirations are combined with courage and commitment, which causes bodhisattvas not to become bored and tired of taking birth in samsara life after life in order to benefit all living beings. In fact, many Mahayana prayers often include the wish to lead every sentient being to enlightenment before one achieves enlightenment. These aspirations and thoughts demonstrate the greatness of the skillful means in the Mahayana.

If we are caught in the activities of samsara, then we are regular sentient beings. Therefore one of the bodhisattva's goals is to not be caught in samsara even if they are in samsara. This is accomplished through the power of wisdom. By the power of compassion, one wishes not to be caught in nirvana. Being caught in nirvana is like personal retirement. You retire from samsara and just enjoy your retirement in nirvana. So through compassion you refuse to retire into your own happiness when others are still suffering. By the power of compassion you continually engage in samsara even though you are free from samsara. These are the principal skillful means of the Mahayana.

Based on these skillful means, Vajrayana practitioners don't simply avoid and eliminate negative emotions. They don't just reject negative emotions out of fear. Instead, they use compassionate skillful means to transform the energy of negative emotions into healing medicine. By maintaining their realization with bodhichitta, courage and commitment, they do not get caught in samsara or nirvana.

Question: Does "habituation" mean that you begin to see everything in the same way as though you were doing the same thing over and over again?

Answer: In Tibetan, habitual patterns are called *bak chak*. Habitual patterns have two aspects: action and intention. Intention always comes first. The second is an action based on an intention. Habitual patterns are when you do something repeatedly, such as thinking and then doing something based on that thought.

Habitual patterns are not always bad. For example, in philosophy when you learn and study at an early age you don't know anything. You cannot even read letters such as A, B, C, D. But a teacher will teach you. You will say "A, B, C," "A, B, C," again and again, and it becomes more imprinted in the alaya. Eventually you begin to say these things naturally. Everyone learns in this way. Knowledge is largely created by habitual patterns. In this way, habitual patterns are understood as developing and learning by becoming familiar something.

Question: Is the alaya sort of like sunglasses? For instance, if you do more and more non-virtuous or unpleasant things, they get darker and darker, making the world look darker and darker? Or is it like a box that's continually shooting out little things which are bad?

Answer: I think the alaya can be understood according to both of these analogies. It is like a pair of sunglasses which makes things appear darker and darker or lighter and lighter. Also, the alaya is like a storage box. Sometimes it is translated into English as a "storehouse consciousness." One side of the storehouse has so many things going in, and from the other end, many things coming out. So it is like big warehouse where many imports come and many exports go.

We can also look at memories. Our discussion earlier this morning is not our present discussion. This present is not this morning. According to the Mind Only school, what we remember now is all registered in the alaya. Between this morning and now, trillions of instances have passed. And that means these instances have completely changed. But still there is the continuation of recollecting. Where does this come from? What is said and heard is all imprinted every moment. This moment of discussion happening right now is being registered in the alaya. At the same time we are exploring what we previously registered in the alaya storehouse. We are bringing these imprints out and registering more. In a way we are filing through our individual alayas and reading the files in the present moment. We are investigating imprints that have already been filed and at the same time we are creating new imprints based on these old files. All of this is happening instantly and at the same time.

Question: Is the seventh consciousness what clings to an individual self or ego? Does it then interpret what is coming from the alaya as belonging to a separate self?

Answer: Yes. In philosophical teachings, the seventh consciousness is generally considered a subdivision of the sixth consciousness. There is no big difference between the sixth consciousness and the seventh consciousness. But the distinction is made between different consciousnesses because the emotions are very distinctive and strong. The mind can project itself externally due to strong emotions. For this reason the seventh consciousness is sometimes called the emotion-consciousness.

In the *Thirty Stanzas*, Vasubandhu says that the seventh consciousness is a combination of nine different mental states which coalesce. First among those nine is the conception of the ego, or the "I." This is the root. One focuses on the "I" and believes in it. Secondly, one grasps and clings onto the "I." Thirdly, there is a feeling of self-importance or pride that one feels about the "I." Then one continually thinks about the "I." Sometimes this is called ego-mania. These are the four mental states that are specifically related to the ego. Then there are five other retinues that are common to all the sense-consciousnesses. These are feeling, conception, touch, thinking and then rethinking. Rethinking is like going over an idea repeatedly. The ego is held together by these nine mental states all of the time, whether this is very obvious or very subtle. The seventh consciousness always functions in this way.

Question: What happens to the alaya upon attaining buddhahood?

Answer: It is said that the alaya transforms or changes and becomes the dharmadhatu wisdom. This includes whatever we register in the alaya up until enlightenment—all the aspirations, prayers, good thoughts. When we reach enlightenment all of this transforms into the dharmadhatu wisdom. The other wisdoms and the three kayas carry this on.

Question: If the alaya transforms into the dharmadhatu wisdom when we become enlightened, does this mean that the alaya is only relatively individual and that once we attain Buddhahood the dharmadhatu wisdom pervades everything?

Answer: Dharmadatu wisdom is pervasive emptiness. However we cannot say that the dharmadhatu wisdom of Buddha Shakyamuni is the same as the dharmadhatu wisdom of Vajrasattva. Even though the dharmadhatu wisdom is open emptiness, this wisdom aspect is very individual and personal to each buddha.

Similarly our alaya is emptiness. Our alaya is pervasive. Yet this doesn't mean that we are all one thing or that we all share one alaya. Mahayana Buddhists do not believe this. The alaya carries its own identity and qualities in a unique way.

Question: So would you say that the uniqueness of the alaya remains when one achieves enlightenment, but that there is no sense of being an individual?

Answer: Yes. Even though it's emptiness, it's unique. On the relative level, each and every buddha's wisdom, aspirations and their fulfillment is quite unique or different from any other buddhas'. But the nature is the same. All of the buddhas and all sentient beings have the same nature of emptiness. But there is a difference when the nature begins radiating and reflecting externally on the relative level. For an enlightened being, the radiating, arising energy of the wisdom of the union of relative and absolute truth shines distinctively, carrying out activities as they are needed. This happens even though everything is empty.

Question: So are you saying then that on the ultimate level there is just the expanse of emptiness, but that on the relative level it manifests in unique beings or unique ways.

Answer: On the absolute level, everything is emptiness. We can't say it is one or it is many. But the absolute truth of emptiness is free from all complexities and all extremes. It is free from labelling and free from conceptions. This means that it is free from the one and free from the many. At this level there is nothing on which you could base any kind of analysis. But on the relative level, when this same nature arises, every individual appears in his or her own unique way.

Question: According to sutra Mahayana and tantra Mahayana, how does the alaya, which is vague and impartial, relate to wisdom mind, which seems to be clear and impartial?

Answer: Firstly, there is no big difference between how the sutra Mahayana and the tantra Mahayana explain the alaya. From the Mind Only school all the way through Dzogchen, the mind is pretty much considered in the same way. Of course in the tantra Mahayana it becomes clearer and brighter. The Madhyamaka school's explanation about the mind is more subtle, and in the Vajrayana teachings it becomes even deeper and clearer. Otherwise, they are the same.

But why is the alaya blocked or obscured? Simply put, even though the alaya is impartial it cannot perceive the past or the future. It cannot go any further than what is happening right in front of it in the present moment. Because of this, it is said to be obscured.

The alaya is impartial because it doesn't discriminate between good, bad, or neutral habits. Whatever you do with it will register it. The alaya does not accept or reject anything since it registers everything.

Question: How is the intellectual mind (*sem*) related to the alaya?

Answer: The sixth consciousness or the mind consciousness comes from the alaya. It is one of the waves or the tides of the ocean of alaya.

Question: Does the alaya continue when we die?

Answer: When we die the five consciousnesses will definitely merge into the sixth consciousness. The sixth consciousness—including the emotion consciousness—will then mostly merge to the alaya. According to the Buddha's teachings, certain situations and circumstances can cause the sixth consciousness and emotion consciousness to come up even we die physically. Sometimes these three consciousnesses—the sixth, seventh and eighth—seem to function as one. Many times the bardo experience is a reflection of the mind consciousness. Teachings on the bardos say that all of our experiences come from the alaya. Only then do we begin to experience anything. This is also true of dreaming.

The *Twenty Verses*

In ancient times, Buddhism flourished in India as a brilliant sun rising in every direction, unobstructed by any clouds or fog. During this peak of Buddhism in India, the great master Vasubandhu was appreciated and honored by all great masters as the "Second Buddha." Vasubandhu taught many different teachings that deal with both the Hinayana and the Mahayana. This particular teaching is a Mahayana teaching on the Mind Only school. The *Twenty Stanzas* explains that everything is mind—actually nothing but mind. In order to bring about this realization, in the *Twenty Stanzas* Vasubandhu explains that everything is mind by using logic, reasoning, scriptural study of the Buddha's teachings.

Lung means "support from the scriptures of Buddha's teaching." *Rigpa (rigs pa)* is "support through the logic and reasoning of one's self or others." By putting these supports together, Vasubandhu establishes that everything is mind. This claim is not just in the Mind Only school. Madhyamaka, outer tantra, inner tantra, and inner Dzogchen are all based on the view that everything is mind. In the Vajrayana, one begins to see that everything is mind. If we don't realize that everything is mind, then we begin to make distinctions between subject and object. We begin dividing. We create divisions in the nature instead of finding the nature's reality. Therefore the Mind Only school's philosophy is essential to all the views of Mahayana teaching. We should remember and think about this. With this understanding, we will now begin studying the root text, *The Twenty Stanzas.*

The explanation of the *Twenty Stanzas* has four parts: The first is the title of the teaching. The second category called the "homage of the translators." The third is the main point of this teaching, or the meaning, and the fourth is the conclusion of this teaching.

Title of the Teaching

There are two titles of this root text—one in Sanskrit and one in Tibetan. The Sanskrit title it is known as the *Vimshatikakarika.* The Tibetan title is *Sumchupa Tsig le'ur jepa.* Both of these titles are translated into English as "The Twenty Verses." This text is a commentary by Vasubandhu himself, which is known as a self-commentary. *Vimsa* means "twenty" in Sanskrit. A *tika* is a commentary. And, *karika* means "stanza or verses." So today we are dealing with Vasubandhu's root text, the *Commentary of the Twenty Verses.* This concludes the first section of the text.

Homage of the Translators

The second section is the homage of the translators, which the translators wrote when they began their work. In English the homage is: "Homage to the Youthful Manjushri," or "I prostrate to the Youthful Manjushri." According to the guidelines or the law of translations, translators always pay homage at the beginning of a text. In ancient times, when the Dharma began to flourish in Tibet, the great King Trisong Deutsen, together with his son and his grandson, made a set of rules on how to translate Buddhist texts. These guidelines were made according to the wishes of other great masters. One of the guidelines is that a translation must always include what is called the "Homage that will identify to which *Pitaka* the teaching belongs". The Tripitaka are the three "baskets" that encompass the Buddha's entire teaching. When translators follow this rule, immediately after reading the beginning of a text the reader will know whether the text belongs to the Sutra, Vinaya or Abhidharma.

According to this rule, when you translate the teachings of the Vinaya, in the commentary at the beginning the translators should put: "I pay homage to the Omniscient or All-knowing One." And when they are translating the sutra teachings, at the beginning of the text before they begin the translation they say, "I pay homage to all the buddhas and bodhisattvas." If you see this particular homage, then immediately you are able to identify that the text is a commentary on the sutras. When you are translating the Abhidharma teaching or the commentaries on the Abhidharma teaching, the guidelines state say you should write, "I pay homage to the youthful Manjushri," so immediately the reader will know that the text belongs with the Buddha's Abhidharma teachings, or that it is a commentary on the Abhidharma. This is known as the "homage that will identify to which *Pitaka* a translation belongs." In this case, the translators pay homage to the Youthful Manjushri. This means that this teaching belongs within the Abhidharma teachings.

Who translated this text? In the eighth century, when the dharma was being translated into Tibetan, there were people who were known as the 108 great translators. Among these great translators there were the most renowned translators, such as Vairochana, Kawa Paltsek, Chokro Lu'i Gyaltsen and Shang Yeshe De. They are very famous. Among these four famous translators, the translator of the *Twenty Verses* is Shang Yeshe De.

Shang Yeshe De was a fully ordained monk. He took the ordination from the great master Shantarakshita. He was also one of the twenty-five disciples of Guru Padmasambhava. In paintings of the twenty-five disciples of Guru Padmasambhava, he is depicted flying in the sky like a bird. On our wall, he is located close to the emanation of Guru Padmasambhava known as Nyima Özer. Shang Yeshe De translated a great number of texts. He translated the *Twenty Verses* from Sanskrit to Tibetan in the eighth century. This concludes the second section of the text.

The Main Teaching

The third section of the *Twenty Verses* is the text itself. The text is divided into three sections. The first is known as "Establishing the reason that all phenomena are no other than mind." The second section uses more detailed logic and reasoning to support the first section's argument that everything is mind. The third section then demonstrates what the benefit is of knowing that everything is mind.

The text actually has twenty-two stanzas. However, it is named the *Twenty Stanzas*. So now we go to the first stanza, which establishes the reason that everything is mind. Our commentary will follow the root text, supported by the great master Mipham Rinpoche's brief commentary on this text in the form of footnotes.

Establishing the Principal Point: All Phenomena are Only Mind

The first stanza, which is four lines long, says that all existing phenomena of the Three Realms—the Desire Realm, Form Realm and the Formless Realm—are merely mind. All existing phenomena are only our inner mind. There is nothing existing outside of this.

What is this then? It merely perceives the images of the mind. Or perceiving that there is nothing really truly existing. All is perceived as mere illusion or as appearances that do not truly exist. That which you perceive is non-existent.

Vasubandhu uses examples to explain this. When you have cataracts in your eyes and you begin to see many different lines or many different hairs in the sky; or, if you press your eye with your finger and you begin to see two moons or two different forms; or when you have jaundice and you begin to see yellow moons, and so forth, these do not really exist, yet you still perceive them. You see that which does not really exist.

This is the first statement by Vasubandhu. Here, great master

Vasubandhu is not just imagining something and I am not just making this up. This was also stated clearly by the great Omniscient One. The Buddha explained this in the sutra teachings when he said, "Oh noble victorious children! You should know in the following way: The whole three realms are no other than the mind. It is only mind." This is what the omniscient teacher said.

In Tibetan, mind is called *sem*. Synonyms of sem are *yid* or *namshe*. *Nampar rigpa* also means mind. So *sem*, *nyid*, *namshe*, and *nampar rigpa* are synonyms. When we say Mind Only, it completely negates the existence of external objects. It is the complete negation of everything except mind itself. Everything is negated or not accepted, except the mind.

Establishing the Principal Point by Reasoning

The next stanza then establishes the reason and logic of the first point. To establish this logically, it can be divided into two more groups. The first is roughly translated as establishing the principal point. The second is certainly establishing the point.

Establishing the principal point can be divided into two more groups. The first division is stating the objection of the opponent. For example, someone may say, "The Mind Only school claims that everything is mind, which is incorrect. This is invalid." When someone debates in this way and provides reasons for their argument, the Mind Only school then argues that such a refutation does not undermine or hurt their philosophy. They provide reasons explaining how their point has not been refuted. This is the second section of the principle point which is called "refuting the objection."

Stating the Objection

How is the Mind Only position refuted? An opponent may say that the whole philosophy of the Mind Only philosophy is going to be completely mixed up if everything is mind and nothing but mind. If there is nothing externally existing besides mind, then how can you ignore that there are so many objects externally? Your mind is not always there. There are so many objects. And because there are so many varieties of objects such as the land and the country, there must also be so many different times. As a result, there would be no certainty of time and no certainty of object if there was only mind. In addition, if everything is your mind then when you look in the eastern direction you would have to see the same thing as when you look to the west. Or maybe you wouldn't be able to see anything at all. Also, time would have be unchanging since there is only one thing—your mind. And if time is not unchanging then certain things would have to happen all of the time. For these reasons, if it is true that everything is mind, then everything would be mixed up in so many ways. And our experience is not like this.

The opponent continues by looking at the Mind Only school's example of a person's vision with cataracts. Of course cataracts cause one to mistakenly perceive many hairs. But these hairs have no activities. They have no function. According to this example, if everything is mind then nothing would be able to happen at all. And nothing could function either. All existing phenomenal objects would become like the hairs of the cataracts. They would not function. Or otherwise cataract hairs would begin to function like existing objects.

Similarly, when we press our finger to our eye we see two moon-shapes. If everything is mind then both of these moons would equally function like the actual moon. Therefore, if you start saying everything is mind, then everything in the whole system will be completely mixed up. Or everything will become lost and disordered. These are possible refutations of the Mind Only school by their opponents.

Refuting the Objection

The great master Vasubandhu provided six different answers to these refutations. Having given a possible refutation, he then proceeds to deny the refutation using logic, reasoning and scripture.

The first response uses the example of a dream. Just like in a dream, even if there are no objects that exist apart from the mind things can still function just fine.

The second response uses everything that you perceive—all objects that seem to exist externally—does not really exist outside of the mind. Vasubandhu supports this with the example of a hungry ghost who perceives water as if it was pus and blood. He uses this to demonstrate that everything that you see does not necessarily exist apart from the mind all the time.

His third response again uses the example of experiences and feelings that happen while one is dreaming. Everything that one does in a dream, as a subject who performs activities in relation to objects, is not always dependent upon things that actually exist external to oneself. In a dream, we can have feelings of happiness or sadness. We can have harmful dreams or beneficial dreams. But none of these experiences are caused by objects that actually exist.

Vasubandhu's fourth answer claims that the sufferings of the three lower realms are no other than visions caused by the appearance of karma. They are one's own karma. This also means that there is nothing externally existing—merely one's own imaginations.

His fifth point is the conclusion that everything is nothing other than one's own perceptions or one's own mind.

The sixth and final point is: where are all of these perceptions arising? Where do these visions come from? They all come from one's own habitual patterns. Everything comes from the habitual patterns of one's own creation.

1. The Dream Example

We will now explain each of Vasubandhu's responses to his opponents in greater detail. The first point is that even though there are no external objects that truly exist in reality, we can still experience things and use things just like in a dream. He explains this point in half of a stanza or less. Opponents of the Mind Only school say that unless something exists outside of the mind everything is going to be mixed up—different time and objects, different lengths and characteristics of mind. But they cannot prove this. This does not change anything about the views of the Mind Only school. The Mind Only school says that everything is like a dream. Even though everything is mind you can still perceive objects. They appear like visions in a dream.

Nothing has to externally exist. Even if everything is mind, things can still function perfectly and in perfect order. Things will not get mixed up. This is similar to what happens in a dream. While dreaming we do not just change from being a man to a woman, from a woman to a bird, and then a bird to a snake. Things don't change that way. Things change in order and we go section by section. When we see a building, we see the windows and the roof. We see land and formations that make up the building. We see all of this. It is not just completely mixed up. It is a completely perfect display of functioning things. Similarly, when the Mind Only school says that everything is mind this is not going to mix up anything like how things function, the sequence of time or formations of land and objects. Everything remains perfectly fine. Therefore everything is mind and yet everything can still function perfectly and orderly.

2. The Example of the Hungry Ghost

Vasubandhu's second point is that everything that you see externally does not necessarily exist. Whatever you see is not just something that exists outside of you that you then begin to see. When you immediately perceive something, whatever object you experience does not really exist as an external object. It is the power of the mind's habitual patterns that cause your own inner circumstances to change the appearance of the external objects that you perceive. What you perceive is not necessarily 100% existing externally. Even if there is nothing outside at all you can still see something. Vasubandhu uses the example of when a hungry ghost sees water. Beautiful, clean spring water is seen by a hungry ghost as pus or a kind of lava. It may seem very dirty. That means that the lava, puss or dirty liquid do not really exist in the clean spring water—there is no pus out there. The water is not really any of these things. But a hungry ghost still sees these things. Therefore, what you see does not necessarily always exist outside of your own perception, i.e., it is possible to see something that is not present outside of one's own mind.

3. Being Harmed in a Dream

The third point is that an actor, activity and the object of activity can function perfectly even if there are no externally existing things. The doer, what you are doing and object of doing does not occur because of something existing externally. It is all happening because of your mind. Even if there is nothing externally existing, mind can have all of those three activities: actor, activity and the object of action. For example, say that in a dream you meet your girlfriend or your boyfriend and you sit together and feel great joy and happiness. You experience this. Then, even if you wake up you still feel happy and joyous. Yet this has nothing to do with anything that is externally existing. It is only mind performing the three aspects of a doer who does something to an object. You can also experience sadness and suffering in a dream. For example, say that somebody comes and robs you in a dream. That person robs you of everything you own and kills your parents or your dear ones and your relatives. Even you are injured. You may try to run away from all of this. When you wake up you feel so upset and scared. Even your heart is beating quickly. Yet again, there was nothing really externally existing that came and happened to you. It was all in your mind. Similarly, happiness and sadness, good and bad; all of this you can experience perfectly even if there is nothing externally existing. This is because of the power of the mind.

This is also the case in the hell realms. There is nothing but suffering and sadness there. All of the five forms of experiences in the hell realms—being chased by iron dogs, iron birds ripping off your skin, being crushed between the iron mountains and burned on hot iron plates. And all of these experiences are not due to externally existing things. These perceptions are the display or reflection of one's own heavy negative karma.

4. Animals in the Higher and Lower realms

Vasubandhu's fourth answer involves a slightly different kind of question. It asks a question and offers answers to this question. Here he focuses again on the three lower realms—the hell realm, hungry ghost realm and the animal realm. The experiences, visions and feelings of both the three higher realms (i.e., human realm, demi-god realm and god realm) and the three lower realms are no other than one's own mind.

Consider the animal realm in particular. Are the animals that are in the higher realms both in the lower realms and the higher realms simultaneously? For example, what about the animals who live in the human realm, like Semo [Rinpoches' dog]? What exactly are the animals who live in the human realm? Do they look like animals, but are really not? Which realm are they in? And what about those animals in the hell realms like iron dogs and iron birds? Are they really in the animal realm still or are they in the hell realm? Just what are they?

In particular, the animals that are seen in the hell realm are not really in the hell realm because they are not really suffering. The hell realm is a place of suffering and the animals that appear there are not really suffering. Therefore, they are not in the hell realm. They do not necessarily even really exist. They are the display of your imagination or the reflection of your own karmic habitual patterns that appear externally.

What about the animals that are seen in the higher realms? These animals are animals. But what you see as an animal—your perception of that animal—is your mind. If there are a hundred people who look at an animal, each and every person experiences their personal perception of the animal. Our eyes are like cameras. When you look at something you do not directly see what you take the picture of. You see the picture created by your eye. If a hundred people look at an animal there will be two hundred different pictures of what appears through two hundreds eyes. What you see is not the seeing of others. The image that you see is not the same thing as the images seen by others. Perception is different for different people. Perception depends on the mind. Therefore everything is perception. This is the same as saying that everything is mind.

5. All Appearances are Only One's Own Perceptions

Vasubandhu's fifth point is that everything is mind. Therefore, everything that you perceive is no other than the perception of your own habitual patterns created by karma. Because of the power of these habitual patterns so many different things can appear. Yet all of this is your mind.

In the hell realms, beings can see so many different things that appear to be solidly existing. They can see hot fire, hot water, hot earth and hot wind combined together in so many different ways. They can see all of these things. Everything seems so solid and tangible. It is so powerful that that is what the hell beings perceive. But there is nothing really externally solidly existing.

The visions of the hungry ghosts is such that even if their surroundings are filled with food, drinks and so many luxurious things, because of the power of their habitual patterns they do not perceive this. Everything becomes completely the opposite. It seems to be exactly what they cannot use. This is due to the power of their imagination or their habitual patterns.

In the animal realm, many animals share the same things that we do as human beings. But what they perceive and what we perceive, even if it is the same object, is completely different. For example, water animals see the water, the sea or the ocean as a place where they can live; a place they can use. That is their home. For us, we can only use water as a drink if we are thirsty or to wash with. But we cannot stay there. Animals are used to eating raw grass. We can't do that. We live in almost the same places and see each other so much. But our way of life, style, and the way of understanding our lives is quite different. We all have such different perceptions. We even look at the same objects that we both need for survival in completely different ways.

In the human realm, human beings share the same Earth. We share common visions. But there are so many differences. Even if we share the same thing we have so many different perceptions—different ways of looking at things. Therefore we often say, "I like this." "I don't like that." "I like this very much." "I don't like that at all." But all of this is not something that really exists externally. It is all existing and changing according to one's own mind. There is nothing that exists externally that directs the mind. Each mind directs the way that things are used and the way that things are perceived as externally existing.

In the gods' realm even though gods are on Earth they see this place in a way completely different from the way we see it. They experience it as something that is completely pleasing; very beautiful, pleasurable and very perfect. When they experience water it is not just like regular water. It is like nectar for them. And even though it is the same water that we drink, we drink water as if it is just water, whereas they drink nectar.

Since all of these points prove that everything is mind, why do you not believe that everything is mind? There is no way that you cannot except the fact or true point that everything is mind.

6. Perceptions Arise from the Power of Habitual Tendencies

Vasubandhu concludes his six responses by arguing that everything that we perceive is no other than the perception of our own habitual patterns. Every perception comes from the habitual patterns that are imprinted or stored in the alaya. Whatever habitual patterns we have, that is what we perceive. We experience according to our habitual patterns. A habitual pattern is registered in the alaya which then begins to reflect outwardly according to how strongly the habitual pattern is imprinted. The more you perceive reality in a particular way, the stronger and more solid your experience seems to you. As you continue to learn a habitual pattern by repeating it many times, gradually you strengthen the habitual pattern. The appearance of external reality slowly changes according to the degree and strength that we develop habitual patterns. This is it: learning, growing, and developing habitual patterns. Habitual patterns will become externally familiar to us and seem more real according to how much we develop habitual patterns and register them in the alaya.

When we look to the mind, reading our own thoughts, we can see that whatever habitual pattern we are connected more with, or whatever we are used to doing more often becomes a little easier to do. It becomes normal and feels more comfortable to us. Everyone feels this way. This shows that everything is based on habitual patterns. No truly existing external object is directing us. We are directing and establishing our own habitual patterns. And they will inevitably be reflected back to us.

Of course this applies to everything. In samsara, in this world, we have many traditions. Almost every country has different traditions and different systems. Each of them believes that its way is very accurate, solid, tangible, true and almost unchangeable. We make this. But who is this? Who made this? Again, there is nothing external that really solidly exists. It is all our mind, the habitual patterns that we make.

Look at Tibet for example. In ancient times—like thirty or forty years ago—what was the way of life there? What did Tibetans always eat? It was always roasted barley flour, butter tea and turnip soup. And again *tsampa*—more roasted barley flour. And sometimes we ate a little meat. That was the everyday food. Morning, afternoon, and evening.

And we were so happy. We really didn't feel like it was insufficient, incomplete, or that we were suffering. We were actually happy with what we ate. And we didn't have clocks or watches. At night time we measured time by butter lamp pots. During the daytime we measured according to the sun's movement. We also didn't have matches forty years ago. We used only flint to start fires. And there were no pens. We used an ink pot with a bamboo pen. And we were perfectly fine. We were perfectly happy with this. We really didn't have any expectations or thoughts about other things than what we had.

Then we arrived in India. In India it's slightly different. There is more food there. Dal and rice, chapati, and many vegetables. But basically everything stands—dal, rice, chapatti, and potato curry, curry, curry, curry. Morning curry, midday curry and evening curry. Indians are so happy with this. They really don't feel that anything is missing or that they need more than that. Everyday, seven days a week, twelve months a year, they are happy with the same food. And most of the people eat food with their hands. (Rinpoche holds out his thumb and index finger.) This is their spoon. This is their fork. That is their serving spoon. And they don't really feel that they are missing anything. They are totally happy and content. They don't feel that they need anything else. This is the way their habits are developed. This is what they do and they're perfectly happy with it.

When we came to the United States of America this whole system became almost like a dream. It was gone—gone with the wind. Here people have completely different habitual patterns and a different way of life. Here they have so many foods. Morning is different. Afternoon is different. Evening is different. Tomorrow they have some completely different food. Morning has to be different. Afternoon has to be different. Evening has to be different. If it is not different because you are tired and sick someone will say, "Everyday is the same thing. What is going on?" That's what I hear. Don't people say that? This is due to the habitual patterns that we develop.

In the beginning when we came to this country, we came with the eating habits of Tibet and India. So even if we ate salad and fruit we really didn't feel like we were eating food. We had to have something completely different like rice, dal, and chapatis. When we ate this we felt that we were eating something. But when we ate salad and fruit we didn't feel that it was food.

The first time we came to the United States was January 10, 1980 in San Francisco. The sponsor for our trip was Dr. Rhoda. I think that she was listed in the early 70's and 80's in a big book called "Who's Who." She was a doctor and one of the first American navy women. She wrote speeches for a navy captain or general. She sponsored us. She lived in Sacramento and she picked us up from the San Francisco International Airport. As we left the airport she asked whether we were hungry. We were a little hungry but we were also a little shy, so we told her that we were fine. Then she stopped in a restaurant. She had some cake and coffee. Again she asked us if we were hungry. Again I told her that we were fine.

Really we thought that when we arrived at her home she would have something to give us. This was a habitual pattern. In the East when you go to someone's home they always give you some food. We had this same thought. When we got to her house we sat on the chair and sofa and talked a lot about where we come from and things like that. At the same time we were kind of wondering when she was going to give us some food or dinner. And then she offered us tea. Just that. She then asked if we wanted some toast. I thought, "Oh we don't need toast because I'm sure we are going to get dinner." So I said "No, no. Not really now." So that's it. And then she told us that she was really tired because she woke up early to come to the airport. She wanted to go to sleep. She showed us our beds and gave us bedding and after that said good night. That night we were very hungry. Of course it was not like the hunger we had when we were traveling from Tibet to India. But the night was long and we didn't sleep much. This is just one example of a habitual pattern.

In the morning we had breakfast. Toast and such things. She did not eat as much as we did. She gave us organic toast and things like that. Of course we had some toast but that didn't really make us full. In Tibet they have a saying: "A small bird flying in a big empty house." By midday we really expected rice and dal but instead we had salad and some bread. But we never really thought of salad as being real food because in India they don't eat salad very much. Occasionally they eat a little bit kind of cucumbers and tomatoes but just as a small side dish. And in Tibet there is no salad, so we didn't have any salad habitual patterns at that time. In the evening time we said that we would like to cook some rice. So we cooked. These are just stories of our habitual patterns.

Now we've really changed. Because of our habitual patterns, salad is perfect. It is very good. When we go in India and Tibetan families invite us to their homes to eat we feel that we're not really eating good food. Now we like to eat salad. We like less oily food.

So really the difference in the way you perceive things depends on the mind. That is why the great master Vasubandhu said that external objects will be perceived according to your habitual patterns.

These are Vasubandhu's six answers to the first point of his opponents. This first point—the objection from the opponent and the six different refutations of the objection—is known as "establishing the principle point." In Tibetan systems of logic this is called *chok chö (phyogs chos)*. *Chog chö* is the philosophy that you represent when you debate.

The Importance of this Teaching

This is one of the most sophisticated and deep philosophical teachings. Often it is said that studying philosophy is like trying to chew a very nutritious, bone marrow. It has a lot of nutrition but is very difficult to chew.

Many times we have said that this is a very special teaching. This teaching is applied from here all the way through the Dzogchen yana. It establishes that everything is mind by using reasoning and logic. The great master Vasubandhu is pointing out this teaching by using common sense. He is not using anything sophisticated beyond conception—beyond this and that. The great master Vasubandhu is standing right in the middle of the conception world and is showing us that everything is mind. Therefore this is really very special and very beautiful. When we establish this view beautifully then we also understand all that is talked about in Dzogchen and by other great teachers.

In the bardo teachings by Guru Padmasambhava it is always said that every bardo experience is nothing other than the reflection of one's own mind. Recognize that all of these visions are no other than the mind. All of this is no other than the mind. This is what is said. There are light, beams of light and sound. All of these are no other than your mind. This is the same thing that Vasubandhu is pointing out.

When we don't recognize that this is our own mind we are distant from reality. We are going away from the truth, wandering in the dilemma world. Generally, throughout all of the teachings of Buddhism everything is like a hallucination. This is true for the Hinayana teachings as well. Even though in the Hinayana teaching doesn't directly point out that everything is mind, they do say that everything is like a hallucination.

In the Abhidharma teachings of the Hinayana it is said that form is like foam, feeling is like clear water bubbles, perception is like a mirage, conception is a banana tree, and consciousness is like a magical illusion. In simple terms, every compounded object is a hallucination. There is no substantial, tangible true existence. This is true for everything. In the Hinayana teaching, all apparent things are established and discovered to be like hallucinations or bubbles.

The Mahayana then adds an additional point regarding partless atoms and partless consciousness. Hinayanists believe that if you don't hold that partless atoms and partless consciousness exist then nothing can function. They argue that all functions will completely stop since they believe that everything comes from partless atoms. And all consciousness is said to be started by a very subtle particle of consciousness. Besides these two points, the Hinayana discovered and established that all apparent phenomena are baseless like a hallucination or like bubbles.

In addition to this point the Mind Only school establishes that everything is mind. That means that everything is emptiness—everything is based on emptiness. There is no substantial solid existence *at all*. Everything is the display of the mind.

Questions and Answers #2

Question: How can we believe Vasubandhu's argument about hell beings seeing water as lava and pus if we don't observe this for ourselves?

Answer: According to our own experience, what do we see? I never saw a hell realm. I never saw the hungry ghosts. I never saw gods and I never saw asuras. I saw some animals and some human beings. And that is what our knowledge is based on. We don't even see all human beings and all animals. I have not seen past lives or future lives. If we give complete authority to our own direct knowledge then definitely we can say that there are no gods, no asuras, no hell realms and no hungry ghost realms. There are only human beings and some animals. We can certainly say this by relying only on our limited knowledge, perceptions, and feelings. It's not really bad to say this because you are completely relying on your own direct perceptions and your senses according to your capabilities.

This system existed in ancient times before Buddhism, and was the Charvaka philosophy. They said that you should only accept what you see and what you feel. Because of this they also said that virtuous deeds do not produce virtuous results, and that non-virtuous actions do not yield non-virtuous consequences. They believed this because we usually do not see the principal results of performing virtuous and nonvirtuous actions. This way of thinking blocks out any possibilities beyond your own knowledge. It goes only as far as your personal knowledge and experience can reach. One of the Charvaka texts says, "Young girl, enjoy this life. Enjoy this life until you die. After death there is nothing. The body merges into the dust of the earth and consciousness disappears. And this time you will come to an end. Therefore, enjoy this life and do whatever you like." This is what this non-Buddhist tradition said. And this is not really unusual. It is based on only believing or trusting in your own knowledge and our own understanding according to your capabilities.

On the relative level, the Buddhist point of view often says that even if you don't see and don't feel certain things, there is much more to see and feel. Our knowledge and our understanding are very limited. Such limited knowledge cannot begin to see very far beyond its own limitations. Therefore it is possible that there are many things that exist that we have not yet personally experienced for ourselves.

This fact is well known by people who look into the subtler levels of consciousness and into deeper levels of knowledge. In the West there are also many people who have seen further than 99% of what other people have experienced. They saw more. Maybe one or two percent saw further than the rest of the population. Buddhism says that there are many more things to see and understand. That is why the Buddha sometimes talked about the third eye. Buddhists believe that there are many extraordinary ways of experiencing reality, and that every sentient being can deepen and expand their present understanding by training their mind. Many great masters and practitioners have witnessed this for themselves. They have experienced the six realms even though the majority of people don't see them. They exist even if many people don't know about them. There are hell beings, hungry ghosts and animals; humans, asuras and gods. Our eyes can see only human beings and some parts of the animal realms. Therefore even though our eyes don't see these things right now, we cannot just ignore other people's claims by denying that there is nothing that exists outside of the boundaries of our knowledge. This is not exactly the case.

When Vasubandhu began to establish that everything is mind he used examples of dreams, not about the hell realms. The first example he uses to support his argument is the dream example. Why did he use this example? Dreams are common to everyone. Nobody can really deny that dreams exist. Only somebody who has never had a dream can say that dreams don't exist. Since the majority of people have dreams, Vasubandhu uses the example of a dream to prove that there are things that can be seen and function even if they do not exist externally. Then he used the examples of cataracts and hairs. Not every being has these. They are a little more rare than dreaming. He also talks about pressing one's eyeballs and seeing moon-shaped images. Only then does he begin to talk about other realms and other types of beings like the hell beings and hungry ghosts. In a way, the examples of the hell realms are his last statement. They are particularly directed towards those who already believe in Buddhism.

Question: It is clear that when we see something and we grasp onto it, making it appear solid, this is a distortion of reality. But is there something out there that we are distorting? In other words, it's like seeing a rope and mistakenly believing that it is a snake. It is not seeing nothing and saying that there is a snake.

Answer: The Mind Only school explains habitual patterns based on the "Three Characteristics" of the "Three Natures" (*tsen nyi sum, mtshan nyid gsum*). The first of the three characteristics is called *kun tag (kun btags)*. This is translated as "labelled phenomena" or "imputed phenomena". The second characteristic is called *zhen wang (gzhan dbang)*. It is translated as the "power of others" or "dependent phenomena". The third characteristic is called *yong drub* (*yongs grub*), which means "originally existing" or "truly existing." In short, the Three Natures are the imaginary, the relative and the absolute, which are otherwise known as imputed phenomena, dependent phenomena and originally existing phenomena.

In the English translation of the *Twenty Verses*, *kuntag* is translated as "conceptual imputations," which are misconceptions of time and the nature of phenomena.

This means that the labels of every system and tradition—no matter what we call them—are just artificial labelling based on one's own conceptions. Where do we put this imputed phenomena or imaginary conceptions? They come from dependent phenomena (*zhen wang*). And then where do we put that labelling into? The labels of relative truth come from the seventh consciousness and the alaya.

So what is *yong drub*—the true meaning or the truly existing? Something can be said to truly exist if it is free from *kuntag*. Originally existing consciousness or self-consciousness is free from all of the imaginary conceptual labels of *kuntag*. This is better explained by the example of a rope that is seen as a snake. Say that you see a striped rope at twilight in an area where there are snakes. When you see the striped rope on the ground immediately you think that it's a snake and you are frightened as a result. The belief that the rope is a snake and the fear that comes as a result is *kuntag*. The rope itself is known as *zhen wang*. From the beginning there was never any snake at all. It was actually just a rope. This is not something that is newly developed since it is always true. This is known as truly existing or *yong drub*.

Similarly, everything what we perceive and whatever we label with conceptions—all of this is *kuntag*. All external objects such as you and me, this and that—all dualistic conceptions based on a frame of reference that includes subject and object are *kuntag*. And who is thinking these thoughts? Who is labelling experience in this way? In simple terms, it is one's own mind. This is dependent phenomena. Yet the mind and all of the labelled conceptions are originally free. The nature of mind is emptiness. This is known as true existence. For this reason, Vasubandhu said in his *Thirty Stanzas* that the Buddha said that everything has always been free from labelled entities. Within consciousness, all labelled things have the nature of complete emptiness or the three natures or *svabhavas*. Everything that appears has the three natures or characteristics.

Question: According to the Mind Only school, how can the mind exist and be empty at the same time?

Answer: According to the philosophy of the Mind Only school, the subtle mind exists. *Sem*, the mind-consciousness does not truly exist.

But the subtle mind does exist. This subtle mind exists although it is empty. Why is mind empty? Because mind is empty of all duality. The Mind Only school does not directly say that the mind itself is empty. They say that it is empty of duality.

Question: So mind is not empty of itself but empty of anything outside of itself.

Answer: That's right. Mind is empty of others. Mind is empty of the dualities. But mind itself is there. This is why we can say that the Mind Only school is within the *Shentong* (*gzhan stong*) approach.

Establishing Pervasive Certainty

In debating, the second step of a properly stated inferential argument is called establishing certainty or pervasion. In technical terms, we call this establishing pervasive certainty or universal concomitance. You must demonstrate that your argument is accurate and true, or universally applicable and certain. Establishing the all-pervasive certainty has three parts. First, you establish the pervasive certainty through the scripture of the Buddha's teaching. Secondly, you establish pervasive certainty by reasoning and logic. After you establish the pervasive certainty through scripture and logic, your opponent gives a counterargument. You then try to refute their counterargument by showing how it does not disprove your point. In Tibetan, this is called *gagpa pang*, or "avoiding the argument".

Establishing Pervasive Certainty by Scripture

Thoroughly establishing your point is very detailed and subtle, making the point in many different microscopic ways. Establishing pervasive certainty by the scriptures of Buddha's teaching can be divided furthermore into three points.

The Ayatanas of External Objects Exist

In order to establish pervasive certainty through scripture, Vasubandhu explains that Buddha said that all of the aggregates exist. All the objects we perceive are there. This statement has meaning. Why did Buddha say that everything exists?

When the Buddha said that the five aggregates and external objects exist, he also said that there are twelve *ayatanas* (*chem che chu nyi, skye mched bcu gnyis*). These ayatanas are the sparking and erupting things which include the six senses (i.e., eye faculty, ear faculty, nose faculty, tongue faculty, body faculty, and conceptual faculty) and six the objects of the senses (form, sound, smell, taste, sensation, and concepts). Altogether there are twelve ayatanas. Why did Buddha teach about the twelve ayatanas? By knowing the twelve ayatanas it is easy to understand the two states of egolessness, otherwise known as the two selflessnesses.

Why did the Buddha teach that all perceived objects and aggregates exist? Buddha said that things exist externally because there are some people that are so attached to external objects that if he immediately said that there are no existing phenomena it would be greatly shocking to them. This would completely reverse them from the path to liberation since they were not yet able to understand this profound meaning. In order to prevent them from rejecting the path the Buddha taught that form and the other aggregates exist.

This is similar to the idea of miraculous birth. Vasubandhu used the example of miraculous birth to help others understand this same point. Miraculous birth is mainly just a name that we use. Actually there is no such thing as miraculous birth. When you say that something is born miraculously, it means that a miracle was the cause of their birth. But this is just a name that doesn't actually refer to something that truly exists. There is no miracle that is the cause of birth. It is just through the power of karma that forms can appear instantly. A miracle does not give birth to individuals. The idea of miraculous birth is only a skillful way to guide and help others by using something tangible—a platform that people can hold and stay on. It is just a name that the Buddha used to help beings be freed from the causes of their suffering.

Similarly, the Buddha spoke about existing things. He said that all of the aggregates exist. Buddha taught in this way merely to help those who are attached. How do we know that the Buddha said this just for the time being in order to help and guide those who are attached? In the Buddha's teaching he said, "There is no self, no beings, and all of this is caused by habitual patterns." The Buddha said that external objects exist based on temporary reasons. When he said that external objects exist, he also said that the twelve ayatanas exist. But the Buddha only said that objects exist externally in order to help other beings. It was a temporary way to help them, nothing more.

The Outer and Inner Ayatanas

In the tenth verse Vasubandhu establishes the scriptural support by three references to the Buddha's teaching. The first reference explains the reason why the Buddha said that external objects exist. Because of external objects the sense fields are affected. The second reference explains that the six external objects and the six sense fields are the outer and inner ayatanas. The third scriptural reference demonstrates that by investigating the twelve ayantanas you can easily discover the emptiness of the ego.

It should be noted that this discussion about the ayatanas is from Mipham Rinpoche's commentary on the *Twenty Verses*, which is not exactly the same as Vasubandhu's commentary or other commentaries on the *Twenty Verses*. Mipham Rinpoche lived during the 19th century. He was one of the great masters and great scholars of Tibetan Buddhism. He was also predicted by Buddha and Guru Padmasambhava. In addition, his words, deeds and scholarly writings are very amazing and unique. He is truly one of the great logicians in Buddhism. His commentary on the *Twenty Verses* is in the form of footnotes which help to clarify Vasubandhu's auto-commentary. For this reason we're using this text by Mipham. Now let us return to the text.

Why did Buddha teach that forms exist and that there are twelve ayatanas—six objects of consciousness and six subjects of consciousness? He said this to prove how mind works. Who sees forms? It is no other than the mind. If there is no mind, who will say there is form? Therefore form is one of the displays or aspects of the way that consciousness works. Due to the six inner aspects of consciousness, the six external objects of consciousness arise. You do not have the six objects of consciousness without the six consciousnesses. It is because of the six different aspects of consciousness that the six objects appear.

There are five senses or sense fields—the eye, ear, nose tongue and body—as well as five sense objects—form, sound, smell, taste and touch. Altogether these are called the ten forms or *chemche* (*skye mched*). These ten forms are the same throughout all of Buddhism, including the Abhidharma teachings and the four philosophical doctrines. These ten forms include every form in the world whether it is big, small or tiny. There are not more or fewer forms than this. All material substances are objects of consciousness which are compounded from partless atoms.

There are twelve ayatanas. So what happened to the other two? In addition to the ten forms there are the mind and the objects of the mind. The objects of the mind are mental forms or imagination. Mental forms are not form. They are not substantial. They're different from the other ten forms.

Here the great master Vasubandhu says that all of these forms come from the same cause, mind. Again, what is form? Form includes everything: the universe; the sun and moon. I mean everything. But where does it come from? What is the cause of all of this? What is the seed of all of this? According to the Mind Only school all of this comes from the alaya. Everything comes from mind even though all of these objects appear to be so different from one another. But it all comes from mind. And that's why it is said according to the Mind Only school that there is the place or universe (*ne, gnas*), the objects of the senses (*dön, don*), and then one's own body (*lü, lus*). Each of these comes from the mind.

How to Easily Discover the Two Egolessnesses

The twelve ayatanas are mainly a discussion of the mind. The great master Vasubandhu is saying that the Buddha taught about form and the twelve ayatanas in order to prove clearly how mind works: how it projects, how it functions and therefore why mind is so important. Once you understand the twelve ayatanas you will easily discover the true egoless state.

Self-ego

What is the ego? Generally speaking, in Buddhism there are two egos: self-ego (*gang zag gi dag, gang zag gi bdag*) and ego of phenomena (*chö kyi dag, chos kyi bdag*). Of course most of us know what self-ego is. It is the one who says, "I'm the one who saw. I'm the one who hears. I'm the one who smells. I'm the one who tastes. I'm the one who really feels and knows." That 'I' which we feel as something that is very important, is known as the ego. Yet even though we say things such as "I'm the one who sees," who is that 'I' really? If we investigate and look for the 'I' then there is nothing more to explain beyond what we will discover. If we really investigate the one who sees and feels, tastes and thinks—all of this—we cannot find anything substantially existing. There is no thinker or seer or hearer that we actually find. When we look at this again using logic and reasoning, investigation and analysis, if we see something that is singular, independent and permanent, then we can say, "Yes, there is something that is substantially real." But if we don't find anything substantially real, then we will have discovered what Buddhism calls egolessness. There's nothing else besides egolessness actually. When you don't find anything, that's it. Then there's no ego. There's no "I." If the notion of an ego and the thinking that follows this idea is not there, then that's it. You just have to say there is no ego. The first type of egolessness is self-egolessness.

Again this is not just a belief. It's not just blindly trusting in something. This is something that we must investigate and analyze and see for ourselves whether it's true or not. If we find an ego then we have to say, 'Yes there is an ego. I found it.' But if we find that it's not there, then that's it. There is no ego. This is the egolessness of self or self-egolessness.

Ego of Phenomena

The second type of egolessness is the egolessness of phenomena.

The ego of phenomena is generally clinging onto something after we name it. First we identify some object and then we cling onto it. For example, when we say 'ocean' we have some kind of picture of an imaginary ocean in our mind and then we think that it is permanent. Or we think, "This is a stone. I see it right in front of me." This happens in the same way with mountains, trees, buildings and so many other things. We externally project these things. Mind labels these objects and we keep these imaginary pictures in our mind, holding onto them. This is known as the ego of phenomena.

Imputed Phenomena

The imaginary pictures that the mind holds onto are called imputed or labelled phenomena (*kuntag*). This is simply translated as "exaggeration." There are so many different kinds of imputed phenomena, such as happiness and sadness, good and bad, dirty and clean, high and low. Exaggeration also includes all of the different types of names, levels, signs, traditions, and different types of systems. All of these are fabricated by the mind. We continue holding a certain image in the mind, grasping onto the image. First the mind creates this image or label. Secondly, the mind pictures this image and then it continues holding and grasping onto this image as if it were real. There is nothing else besides this. That is why this is called imputed phenomena or exaggeration. Exaggerations function like a striped rope that someone mistakenly perceives as a snake. Someone thinks that the rope is a snake and then repeatedly keeps this image in mind. Yet, the snake doesn't exist at all. It is imaginary. Believing that the snake really exists is known as "exaggeration."

Dependent Phenomena

So what is the base of these imaginations or exaggerations? Where do imputed phenomena come from? The Mind Only school says that they come from consciousness or mind. Of the eight consciousnesses that we have already discussed, exaggerations come from the alaya-consciousness (*kün zhi nam par she pa, kun gzhi rnam par shes pa*). It is the base of all imagination and exaggerations. We translated it as "dependent phenomena."

The Fully Established Nature

Do imputed phenomena exist in the alaya-consciousness from beginningless time? According to the Mind Only school, they do not. They are all temporarily arisen. They are all exaggerations. None of the imputed phenomena really exist. They are all just clinging and grasping. Therefore the self-aware consciousness that is free from exaggerations and imputed phenomena from beginningless time is known as the fully established. In Tibetan this is called *yong drup*. When you free the alaya-consciousness from all of the exaggerations then you discover nature as it is. This is known as realizing the egolessness of phenomena. This brief explanation of the scriptural support is now completed.

Now we will establish Vasubandhu's main point of debate through logic. In order to establish this through logic first we will give a brief explanation on Tibetan Buddhist logic and then a more detailed explanation on the particular points under discussion in Vasubandhu's text.

Vasubandhu is the one of the greatest Buddhist masters. It is said that he was a great lion among the lion scholars. He wrote many teachings that thoroughly explain the different levels of the Buddha's teachings. Vasubandhu's teachings are generally categorized into two groups: commentaries on the Buddha's teachings and secondly, his direct knowledge, which includes knowledge based on logical reasoning. Among these two groups, Vasubandhu wrote this teaching based on his own knowledge, which utilizes logic and reasoning to clarify the teachings of the Buddha.

In the main body of the teaching, he first establishes the point that everything is mind. After establishing that everything is mind, he refutes possible objections by using logic and reasoning. Another way to say this is that in the main body of the teachings first he establishes the main point. Secondly, he establishes this point using logic and reasoning. Thirdly, he explains the purpose of establishing that everything is mind.

We have already completed the first section which establishes the point that is going to be proved. Now we are in the process of going over the teachings that will establish this point through logic and reason. Establishing the main point through logic has two parts: establishing the point by logic and establishing certain pervasion (i.e., universal concomitance) by logic.

Tibetan Buddhist Logic

In Tibetan Buddhist philosophy, a logical argument consists of three parts: subject or *chokchö (phyogs chos)*, pervasion or *jechab (rjes khyab)*, and counter-pervasion or *dokchab (ldog khyab)*.

The Subject of an Argument

Chokchö is roughly translated as the subject of the argument. For example, two people debate about a vase. The debate is not about the vase itself but about the quality of the vase. One says that the vase is permanent and other says that the vase is impermanent. Both of them put forth their reasons for why it is permanent or why it is impermanent. In this way the vase is subject of the debate. This is known as *chogchos*—the subject of the debate.

To continue with the example, one asks for the reasons and logic behind why her opponent says that the vase is impermanent. The other one responds by saying that the vase is impermanent because it is composite or compounded. Being compounded is the logic used to prove that the vase is impermanent. Is it true that if it's compounded it is impermanent? Both debaters have to think about whether this is a true reason or a merely superficial reason. Is this really logical or does this just seem logical? They have to think about this. Of course logic is not something in which we have to believe blindly. We have to find out whether the reasoning is really true or not. In Buddhism we should not just believe or trust in something without investigating it until we have an understanding of the direct knowledge of the phenomenal system as it is. If something is compounded due to causes and conditions then it is impermanent. It is momentary. If there is something that you find that is compounded and is still permanent, then the opponent will have to present this argument. This is how a debate would go.

You must see whether the vase about which there is debate is really compounded or not. When it falls does it break into pieces? If it does it must be impermanent. In this case, proving that it is impermanent is the reasoning behind the subject of the debate. This is known as *chogchö drub*. This means that you have concretely established the subject of the debate. It is inevitably and irresistibly established. When this reasoning and logic corresponds perfectly with the subject of the debate this is known as *chogchö drub*. *Drub* means "now completed." The subject of the debate is now completed or completely established.

Pervasive Certainty

And now you have to examine whether, if it is compounded, it is really impermanent. Is this certain or not certain? Again you have to investigate this. You have to think. If you clearly see that if it is compounded then it is definitely impermanent this is known as *jechab drub*. You have completely established the pervasive certainty. This is true in all cases. It is true for everything that if it is compounded it is impermanent. Pervasive certainty is established.

Counter-pervasive Certainty

Once the pervasive certainty is established, you have to think about *dokchab*. *Dokchab* means counter-pervasive certainty. You have to see whether the opposite claim of the certainty pervasion is true as well. Permanence is the opposite of impermanence. So the counter-certainty pervasion is that if something is permanent , then it cannot be compounded. If something is permanent, certainly it is not compounded. An example of this is the sky or space. Space is not compounded and therefore it is permanent. And if something is compounded then it must be impermanent, like a house or a tree, a mountain or any human being.

In the case of the Mind Only school, Vasubandhu establishes the subject of the debate: everything is mind. In order to prove that everything is mind he uses many different reasons or pervasions such as using examples of one's experience while dreaming as well as all the different visions of the different types of beings in the six realms.

When we look at Vasubandhu's *Twenty Verses* we can see how he perfectly used two types of evidence to support his arguments. One is known as logical support. The other is scriptural support. Scriptural support is always argued last since in general it is only convincing if you believe in the teaching of the Buddha. Yet Vasubandhu argued these points with everyone—Buddhists as well as the non-Buddhists. Therefore, for the Buddhists he also needs to show that he is not just making things up and going outside of the boundary of the Buddha's teachings. He is perfectly maintaining the streams of the Buddha's teachings. To prove this he uses the Buddha's own words.

In a way, it is perfectly fine if you don't believe in Buddhism. Vasubandhu first proves that everything is mind through logic. He proves it through the example of a dream. Everybody dreams—both Buddhists and non-Buddhists. He uses logic to prove that everything is like a dream. Even if there are no external, solidly existing things we can still view everything as a dream.

In general, according to Buddhism we should not believe in the words of the Buddha just because the Buddha said them. We must investigate and analyze what he said and find out whether it is true or not. First we use logic to investigate a point until it is proven to be true. Comparing our results with Buddha's teaching reveals that Buddha was very accurate. In Buddhism we say that Buddha is the "Emperor of the Intellectuals" or "King of Logicians". Among all the intellectuals and thinkers, psychiatrists, and physicists, he is the top. In Buddhism when you start studying philosophy you must use logic to prove the validity of the Buddha's teaching. You should not believe and trust in Buddha only because of your devotion. In a philosophical debate this attitude does not really apply. An argument is not convincing just because you believe in the Buddha. Therefore, you must sort things out with the intellect. If you don't believe, don't know and don't trust and you just close your eyes and presume something to be true—this is not logical. It is incorrect. Just believing in some theory without investigating your assumptions will not help you to discover the real nature of phenomena.

For this reason the very famous logician Acharya Dharmakirti says in one of his teachings that we can only accept what the scriptures say after we apply logic and reasoning. Only logic and reasoning can fully establish whether the teachings of the Buddha are correct or incorrect.

Valid and Invalid Cognition

We must establish what is true and what is not true. In Buddhism, truth can roughly be translated as "valid cognition." There is valid cognition and invalid cognition. Valid cognition is when something is perfectly understood according to the nature of phenomena. If something is not perfectly aligned with the nature of phenomena and therefore is outside of the nature of phenomena, it is invalid cognition. According to Buddhism valid cognition is the reality of the nature of relative truth or of the absolute truth. To bring this forth clearly as it is, is called *tsema* (*tshad ma*) in Tibetan. In Sanskrit this is known as *pramana. Tsema* and *pramana* are translated as valid cognition.

Direct Valid Cognition

In simple terms, there are two types of valid cognition: direct valid cognition and inferential valid cognition. Direct valid cognition is something that we see, hear, smell, taste or touch. For example, if an eye perfectly sees a form or an ear hears a sound exactly as it is, this is direct valid cognition. The same goes for other sense faculties: there is direct valid cognition if a nose smells a smell exactly as it is, a tongue tastes exactly what a taste is, and body-consciousness experiences a touch precisely as it is.

There are four direct valid cognitions. The first is known as the direct valid cognition of senses. The second is direct valid cognition of mind. The third is the direct valid cognition of self-awareness. And the fourth is direct valid cognition of meditators or of the yogis or yoginis.

Direct Valid Cognition of the Senses

What is the direct valid cognition of the senses? This is when the five senses function perfectly without any mistakes.

Direct Valid Cognition of the Mind

Direct valid cognition of the mind is the unobscured, undeluded mind. It is like a blank mind that begins analyzing whatever object it perceives.

Direct Valid Cognition of Self-Awareness

What is the direct valid cognition of self-awareness? This is demonstrated by one's own feelings. You don't have to ask to anyone about your feelings. Whatever you experience you will know it yourself. If you feel bad, you will feel bad perfectly. If there's happiness, you will feel happiness perfectly. This is true and accurate, and is therefore known as direct valid cognition of the mind.

Direct Valid Cognition of Meditators

And then what is the direct valid cognition of meditators, yogis and yoginis? This is the vision and realization of the practitioner. The direct valid cognition of a realized practitioner goes beyond the other three direct valid cognitions. We cannot fit the direct valid cognition of a meditator within the boundaries of the other direct valid cognitions. This goes further, deeper, and is stronger and sharper. It goes to the past including past lives. It goes a far distance into the future. It goes to the different realms here and now. With the direct valid cognition of a meditator one can see gods, nagas, any invisible being and every visible being. This type of direct valid cognition depends on one's realization and the degree of one's power. The direct valid cognition of the meditator goes further than our tiny other valid cognitions. We should not expect to fit everything into our pocket.

Great masters have this type of direct valid cognition. For example, Guru Padmasambhava predicted in the 8th century the events of the 19th and 20th centuries. How did he do this? If we doubt that he could do this just because we cannot do this—and we cannot even see the events of tomorrow—we are putting too much authority in our own limited direct valid cognition. These great masters have more knowledge. This we see even in the human realm. Some people have more knowledge than others. Everyone's knowledge is not exactly the same. But just because you don't see something you cannot say that what someone else sees is completely untrue. This is incorrect. Therefore, even though we depend on our limited knowledge we cannot completely block out what is outside of our own knowledge. If we do this we are shrinking our knowledge. We are closing our boundaries.

In brief, the great logician master Dharmakirti said that the direct valid cognition of a yogi or yogini is completely inconceivable to the other limited direct valid cognitions. He continued by saying that it is not logical to argue that something does not exist just because you do not see it. Just because you believe that something doesn't exist doesn't mean that this is true. This type of reasoning is not logical.

In Buddhism there are these four direct valid cognitions. The third one—the direct valid cognition of self-awareness—is what we mostly have. The fourth type only occurs for those who have realization. At this time most of us have only the first three direct valid cognitions. But of course who knows—maybe you have the fourth one too! The Buddha also said that we cannot know what other people's degree or level of realization is unless we are fully enlightened. Therefore, don't make commentaries about others.

Inferential Valid Cognition

The second type of valid cognition is inferential valid cognition. Inferential valid cognition is not a direct valid cognition. It is behind it. Using direct valid cognition as the base of our reasoning, we begin to discover inferential valid cognition. True direct valid cognition is necessary to discover inferential valid cognition. Without the true reason of direct valid cognition we cannot bring about inferential valid cognition.

Inferential valid cognition has many divisions. We won't go over all of them in detail, but one simple way of understanding inferred valid cognition is looking at the result. By investigating the result you develop a more clear understanding of the cause.

For example, on the far side of a mountain you may say that there is a fire. Even though you don't see any fire directly you can infer that there actually is a fire behind the mountain. What is the reasoning or logic behind this? You see smoke. Through the direct valid cognition of smoke you infer the existence of fire. This is an example of a true inferential valid cognition.

Now you have to think about whether there is ever any smoke without fire. If you find an example of smoke without fire then you cannot be sure that you have a true inferred valid cognition since the smoke may be caused by something other than fire. You also cannot say that there is fire because you see something that looks like smoke. There are many things that look like smoke. You cannot prove that there is fire if you do not know whether or not what you see is actually smoke.

In general, what is the relationship between fire and smoke? Logically, one is the cause and the other is the result. Fire is the cause of smoke. In Buddhist logic, inferential valid cognition applies to everything that is not direct valid cognition. For example, say that your life is quite beautiful and nice. You are experiencing the direct valid cognition of a beautiful life. The direct valid cognition is the result. This beautiful life has a cause even if we don't see it directly. But the result—

a good life—we see in the state of direct valid cognition. And since everything happens due do causes and conditions, according to Buddhist logic it follows that in a past life you must have done something good. It must have been good since your life now is good. This type of understanding is roughly translated as true inferential valid cognition.

Scriptural Valid Cognition

The third type of support is scriptural valid cognition. In a way it is a subdivision of inferential valid cognition. Scriptural valid cognition is completely beyond direct valid cognition and inferential valid cognitions. Since it is completely beyond these valid cognitions it is difficult to understand according to time and distance. It is so subtle that we can't really figure it out. In order to investigate and analyze this we use logic known as the inferential valid cognition of scripture.

Scriptural valid cognition involves some degree of making assumptions. You must examine the Buddha's teaching to see if it is true or not. What the Buddha said about the state of direct valid cognition is not contrary to our experience. It is accurate. What Buddha said about inferential valid cognition is also not contradictory. It is perfectly true. Is what Buddha said when he began teaching and what he said at the end of his lifetime true? Do these teachings support one another or are they contradictory? Do his later teachings negate his earlier teachings or do they overlap with one another? When we look closely we discover that that there are no contradictions in the entire range of Buddha's teaching. Once you recognize this you can trust his teachings, knowing that they must be true. There's nothing more that we can do because our knowledge is limited, unless we have direct yogic valid cognition. Then it's definite. But otherwise we have to rely on something and that is why scriptural valid cognition is necessary. In this way, because whatever the Buddha said about the nature of relative and absolute truth was true we can infer that the whole range of his teachings must also be true. We use his words to help us determine the truth of whatever we are investigating.

This is a general outline of the Buddhist system of logic. There are three guidelines to debate: *chogchö*, *jechab*, and *dokchab*. These are the guidelines and the framework of any debate. They are not just saying whatever they want and then their opponent says the opposite. Within these guidelines, if an argument is incorrect the opponent will try to prove this. If it's correct then both will agree. This is generally how debating works.

The teaching of these great masters is totally based on this system of logic and reasoning. It is not just based on belief or what sounds good or by assuming that what the Buddha said was true without any investigation.

Establishing Pervasive Certainty by Reasoning

This is a teaching on atoms. On the relative level, the ultimate cause of forms are atoms. As we said before, every form is included in the *ten forms*. There are not more than ten forms and there are not less than ten forms. The ultimate cause of all of these forms is atoms. Here the word 'atom' means an indivisible particle. In Buddhism, an indivisible particle is called a "partless atom" or *dultren chame* (*rdul phran cha med*). It has no parts so it cannot be broken into smaller pieces. In other words it is indivisible.

Why is great master Vasubandhu using logic to debate about atoms? In Buddhism, the first two of the four major philosophical schools—Vaibhashika and Sautrantika—believe that the ultimate cause of the ten forms is atoms. Not only do these two schools believe this but generally in the world the great thinkers believe that all forms develop from some subtle state of atoms or small, indivisible particles. This is common knowledge for most human beings. Therefore Vasubandhu uses logic to refute this point in order to bring us to the realization of emptiness.

Vasubandhu offers four arguments that refute the existence of indivisible atoms. If the ten forms do not have an ultimate cause then they cannot exist as a result. By refuting the true existence of the ten forms Vasubandhu aims to prove that everything is mind.

First Vasubandhu presents his opponent's point of view: If there is mind and there are forms then it is impossible that everything is mind. In response, master Vasubandhu asks his opponent whether or not it is true that forms must come from atoms? If forms come from atoms, then what are these atoms like? Do they have parts or not?

The Sautrantika and Vaibhashika schools believe in the existence of partless atoms. But how can partless atoms be perceived by the eye-consciousness? If they have no parts, how can they be perceived? It cannot become an object of the eye. Some philosophers say that they can be seen because even though they are partless they have parts. It is partless with parts. Master Vasubandhu argues that such a view is not acceptable. One is just playing word games. If atoms are partless then they cannot have parts. So how can they be perceived?

When we see something it is not just made up of one atom. There have to be trillions of them, countless atoms. And since there are so many atoms, how can the eye consciousness see all those countless atoms? The eye consciousness will not see each of those countless atoms. If you think that all of these countless atoms are put together, they cannot become one atom because each atom has different components or elements. This is Vasubandhu's brief refutation of partless atoms.

Unitary or Multiple Atoms Cannot Be Combined

Vasubandhu's first argument against the existence of partless atoms is that six partless atoms cannot join together to form one partless atom. Generally speaking, when the universe began to form, many atoms came together. When we speak of the six subtlest types of atoms we are mainly just using them as an example. So many atoms have to come together to form larger objects. So why are there said to be six subtlest atoms? Why six? Six is an easy number to use as an example because there are four directions—north, south, east and west—as well as up and down. When an atom comes together with other atoms its sides touch every direction. So here we use the six directions as an example of this.

The one atom in the center begins coming together with six other atoms of the same type in order to create a larger form. Vasubandhu then asks whether, when these six other atoms come from the different directions to the central atom, they contact one another or not? Do they touch or do they not touch? If the six different directions touch the central atom then what is called a partless atom cannot really be partless since it has parts. It has at least six sides. If it is partless, than how can it have at least six different parts?

If there is no contact between the central atom and the other six atoms then how can they come together to form larger, more apparent objects? It would almost be like the atoms were falling into a black hole. Billions and trillions of atoms could come together but all of them would fall into one another like the sky merging into the sky. How could it ever come together to create larger forms? Therefore, by using logic we can see that partless atoms do not exist and that they cannot come together in any way whatsoever.

Questions and Answers #3

Question: When you were in shedra how did you learn to debate?

Answer: We memorized the root texts and commentaries, as well as the system of logic of the three parts of an argument that we mentioned earlier (the subject of a debate and arguments for pervasive certainty and counter-pervasive certainty). Of course there were many other things to memorize, but the rest comes when you debate and when you need it, it kind of comes by itself.

The person who makes an argument sits down on the floor on a cushion, and his or her opponent stands up as he or she debates the point. The one who is sitting establishes the subject of the debate by making an argument. If someone else doesn't agree with this point or wants to debate, he or she gets up and tries to refute the point.

The debating systems in Tibet where people clap their hands and move their feet while making different sounds started around 11th century under the influence of a very famous master known as *Chapa Chökyi Senge* (*phya pa chos kyi seng ge*). Chapa Chökyi Senge was one of the very famous logicians in Tibetan Buddhist history. In ancient times in India, before the 11th century, they had Buddhist debate but they didn't necessarily get up and clap hands and feet and use their malas, and all of that. They just sat down face to face and debated. This system continues to be maintained in all of the four schools of Tibetan Buddhism, which include the Kadampa, Nyingma, Kagyu and Sakya schools. It became especially very popular and promoted when the Gelukpa school appeared in the 14th and 15th century.

Question: Are logic and the rules of logic merely imputed phenomena?

Answer: Yes. According to the absolute point of view they are exaggeration.

Question: And from a relative point of view, logic is just the best way to handle conventional phenomenon?

Answer: Yes. On a relative level there are two systems of meditation. One is a scholarly type of meditation. The other is more based on practice and devotion. These are the two ways to practice. But if you like to practice the more intellectual, scholarly way, then the best way is to debate using logic. This will concretely establish knowledge of the nature of reality. Of course there is also the simpler, devotional way of practicing.

For example, Milarepa told to Gampopa not to waste his life on words and analysis. He told him to give up these things and engage in recognizing the absolute truth. And this was not just Milarepa. Many other great practitioners also said this. According to the more devotional way of practicing you trust the words of your teacher or the Buddha and then you just begin to practice.

Question: If everything has a habitual pattern of the mind, how can something like logical consistency function among so many different minds?

Answer: Logical consistency functions between different human beings because human beings share similar karmic vision or karmic attitudes. We have the same kind of senses. Our eyes are aligned almost the same, but some are blue and some are green or black. All of our systems are basically similar—our nose, tongue, ears and skin are all pretty much the same. Our sense organs are similar. Since the structure of our sensory systems is karmically similar, we have the tendency to perceive things in a similar way. Therefore, even though at certain levels there are differences, at the gross level we pretty much share eighty or ninety percent of the same ways of experiencing external reality. Logic developed based on these similarities among humans.

Question: The dream example seems to be very important to proving the position of the Mind Only school. Could you please explain more about the similarities between dreams and apparent reality?

Answer: Let's say that we are dreaming now. And while we're dreaming now we see the land and buildings, men, women and children. We also hear things, say things, speak with others and walk around. At the same time we also have feelings: good feelings, bad feelings and neutral feelings. Because of these feelings we have hopes and we have fears. All of this feels very real. It seems that this is truly happening. It's not something that we're imitating or experimenting with. I mean it seems that we're truly experiencing what is truly happening. But the moment we wake up, the whole universe of our dreaming experience completely disintegrates. It is gone.

Similarly, during the daytime when we're not dreaming everything is the same as when we are dreaming. We see the land and buildings. There are men and women talking. Everything appears in the same way. According to Mind Only school this is the dream. Even though it looks so real and feels so true and so solid, it is nothing other than a dream.

When we are dreaming in the world we are in the sleeping state of ignorance. In this ignorant state we are sleeping and all of this is a dream. We will wake up and all of this will completely change when we finish the ignorance—when we wake up from ignorance. When we finish the ignorance we will have completed all of these dreams. These dreams will be gone. The dreams of our exaggerations based on relative truth will entirely disappear. At this point, the Mind Only school says that a pure dream will arise. The effect of impure dreams comes to an end by eliminating its cause: the impure power of others or impure dependent phenomena. This happens once our meditation practice removes these impure perceptions. Then the pure dream of the pure dependent nature will appear. This is called pure vision or the pure displays that are experienced by buddhas and tenth bhumi bodhisattvas. Ultimate pure vision is the vision of the Buddha. Of course this is not only in the Mind Only school, but in all of the schools from the Mind Only school all the way to Tantrayana. Vajrayana and this teaching are basically the same except they use different terminologies. The meaning is the same.

All of the experiences of this life are like a dream. Compared to when we were young, our vision, thoughts and understanding are now quite different. What we think now and what we used to think almost disprove one another. It is just like a dream. Even in this lifetime we have gone through many different stages of dreaming. This is why the Mind Only school says that we are constantly in a dream state. Just as old dreams cease, new dreams ignite. We are in an ongoing, unfolding dream state. These teachings can be used to bring about realization more clearly in the Vajrayana teaching.

The bardo of dreaming is nothing than discovering that everything is like a dream. I mean, it is dream. In the Vajrayana teachings, there are techniques that are used specifically to come to this realization. In Vajrayana teachings, it often states to practice on dream. By doing this, we can bring more of the realization of nature just as it is, more quickly. Often in the teachings it is said that all of our experiences are like memories of the past. How many people have we known from when we were young until now? In how many places did we stay? How many things did we eat? How many different things did we discuss? Many of them have disappeared. It is almost the same as being gone. This is the same as our dreams. There is no really big difference. All of our dreams of the night before are now just memories of what is now gone. The experiences in our dreams are only in our memories. There isn't even a trace of their existence left. Our experiences are gone as though we have woken from a dream.

For this reason, the Buddha taught in the *Prajnaparamita* teachings that all existing phenomena is like a dream, magic and a mirage, even this mind. How many times have we already changed our mind? We have changed from a child's mind to a mid-teenager's mind, and into a grownup mind. How many times has the mind changed, disagreed with itself and disproved of its own memories? This happens with our very own mind. This shows that mind itself is like a dream.

Question: What are the differences between the dreams we have at night and our dream-like waking experience?

Answer: According to the teaching, dreams during the night and waking dreams are both dreams. There are really no major differences. But there is one smaller difference. The daytime dreams are heavily habituated and the night time dreams have lighter habits. Thus, one habit is light and the other habit is heavy. Dreams are heavy during the day because we already have heavily formed physical habits within the waking dream. Because of these solid habits of physical reality our senses also appear to exist concretely. This causes a very solid and heavy habit of communication between the sense fields and the objects of the senses. Therefore when the object is heavy, the physical is heavy, the senses are heavy, and the communication with the objects of the senses are all heavy, even if you think that everything is just a dream it won't help immediately due to the heavy obscurations or heavy habitual patterns.

The dreams that we have while sleeping are usually not so heavily laden with habit patterns. The moment you are aware you are dreaming, the dream may shift. Other than that, dreams we have at night and our dream-like waking experience are dreams. There is really no difference between the two kinds of dreams. One is based on heavier habits and other comes from lighter habits.

Generally what does a habit pattern mean? A heavy habit is something that we strongly grasp it. We don't grasp at dreams too much, but we do grasp at physical things very much. Whichever birth we take, whichever form we take, we hold onto our daytime waking visions of physical things. We grasp at them so strongly. Therefore, it makes these habits stronger and more difficult to change. If you have the same realization as the buddhas and bodhisattvas, then you can easily change these patterns. Even these things happening in the waking status can be changed. Even if it looks like the same things happen to buddhas and bodhisattvas which sentient beings experience, inwardly they are not experiencing the suffering and difficulties in the same way as ordinary beings.

For example, the magician Bhadra invited the Buddha to the lunch in Rajagiri and offered a magical display of lunch. According to the teaching it was completely magical. There was no actual food. But then the buddha transformed these magical appearances into food for the monks and nuns who were with him. He changed the magical display into what would suit the needs of beings due to their grasping. He then blessed the food and at the end of performing dedication prayers he said, "Magical Bhadra offered magical food to the magical Buddha and his disciples. May magical Bhadra achieve magical results."

After he said this the magician Bhadra felt very upset and sorry for what he did. He saw that the Buddha knew that he had tried to trick him. He went to the Buddha thinking that he had done terrible things and asked for forgiveness. The Buddha told him not to be worried. He said that everything was magic, and that he had not done anything particularly exceptional.

Question: Let's say an astronomer suddenly discovers a new star. In both cases, a dream and a scientific discovery, a feeling of surprise emerges from the mind. Why does this happen if the mind is habitually patterned?

Answer: Everything is mind. It is all produced by the mind. Whether scientists discover a new planet or whether you have an unusual nightmare or dream, all of this is mind-made. I'm sure that scientists will discover more new planets and I'm sure that we will have more dreams and nightmares. All of this is a dream. All this is mind. And mind is infinite. Mind is vast. We are not talking about mind as if it is some small object like a grain of rice. Mind is infinite. Mind is vastness. Mind is open. Mind is emptiness. Therefore, anything can come and it will still be mind.

Question: Let's say there is a universe with no sentient beings and it hasn't yet been discovered. If everything is mind, how could this universe exist if we don't know about it? Does it exist because the Buddha knows about it?

Answer: According to Buddha's teachings, there is hardly any space where there are no sentient beings. There are sentient beings as far as there is space.

When scientists take photos of the planet Mars for example, they usually don't find any sentient life. This is what they believe. It's true that scientists have not discovered life on Mars. But according to Buddhism, that doesn't really prove that there are no sentient beings there.

"Sentient beings" refer to those who have mind, consciousness, or feelings and senses. Sentient beings do not always have physical forms. In Buddhism, there are visible beings and invisible beings. Invisible beings cannot be detected and can barely be detected by binoculars or by photographs. Maybe there are sentient beings without any gross level physical existence that a camera cannot catch. Or perhaps sentient beings really do not exist on Mars.

Question: Does the word "sentient" have two different meanings? Sometimes sentient seems to mean all the things that are attached to our alaya. At other times "sentient" seems to mean the conscious experience that we are having.

Answer: In Tibetan, "sentient being" is *semchen (sems can). Semchen* is usually translated as "sentient being" or sometimes just "being." What does *semchen* mean? *Sem* means mind or the mental consciousness. *Chen* is a possessive. So whoever has mind or whoever has consciousness is called *semchen.*

What is mind? Of course the senses depend on organs in order to function. According to Buddhism those that have mind must have the sixth consciousness, the emotion consciousness, and the alaya. They must at least have these three consciousnesses in order to have mind. The other five consciousnesses (i.e., the five sense-consciousness) are not necessary in order to have mind. This is why it is possible for a sentient being to exist without a physical body.

The sixth consciousness is like a self-projection of the alaya. The alaya's principle hub is the sixth consciousness, the conceptual consciousness of the mind-consciousness. From the mind consciousness, one's experience begins to be reflected according to what the five senses are doing. The eye, ear, nose, tongue, and body are like five stations which receive signals from your surroundings. According to the philosophy of the Mind Only school there are many details to each of these processes.

For example, when the eye sees a form, what the eye sees the very first instant is the actual form or body. But the next instant, the message has already been received by the central hub of the mind-consciousness; the form has already gone to the sixth consciousness. At this point the mind-consciousness is already controlling almost everything. It kind of deludes the instant state by duplicating an image of the original form that was seen. The first instant was really the form. After that it is just an image in the mind-consciousness. This same basic process can be applied to all of the other sense-consciousnesses as well—sound, smell, taste and physical sensations.

The hub of the mind-consciousness is very powerful. The five senses only exist in the present moment. They only go as far as the present. But the sixth consciousness goes throughout the three times. It goes to the past, the present and the future. It is very powerful and very profound. The five sense consciousnesses contact the actual forms in the present moment. The sixth consciousness interprets this information according to how it is habituated.

At certain times the sixth consciousness merges back into the alaya. This happens when you suddenly become very drowsy. The mind-consciousness is dissolving into the alaya. This also happens when we faint or become totally unconscious. At that time the mind merges into the alaya.

Arhats and meditators are known to achieve profound states of concentration (*snyoms 'jug)* in which the sixth consciousness merges into the alaya. During a very good shamatha meditation, the conceptual mind mostly returns to the alaya. Otherwise, the sixth consciousness is always active. It's almost always very busy.

Question: How do we know when we have a valid cognition? How do we know we're not being fooled by the alaya?

Answer: Deep down, every valid cognition arises from the alaya. But since alaya has no partialities, it does not really influence or change the valid cognitions. The valid cognition is more like the sparking state of the alaya or consciousness. Therefore the alaya won't really delude or manipulate a valid cognition. It will just see what things are there. Even though it's mind, it will perceive things commonly seen and commonly agreed upon by most everyone. Therefore, that really won't influence or change the valid cognitions.

The system of valid cognitions can be analyzed and explained by the mind-consciousness. But even if the sense consciousnesses and mind-consciousness are active, they are not going to change the valid cognitions. It will be as it is.

Question: From the Madhyamaka perspective would the Mind Only school be seen as the extreme view of eternalism?

Answer: No, Madhyamaka doesn't really see the Mind Only school as extreme. But, according to the point of view of the Madhyamaka, the Mind Only school has errors. In one way, these errors are small. The Mind Only school says that self-awareness exists free from all dualities. While both schools agree that there is awareness, the Mind Only school argues that self-awareness exists in a concrete, solid way. For the

Madhyamaka, this is considered to be a mistake. According to the Madhyamaka point of view there is no concrete solid existing awareness at all. Besides this, most Madhyamaka philosophers say that there are not really any extremes in the Mind Only view. Of course, when Madhyamaka explains its own school and the Mind Only school, technically they use the system in slightly different ways. Otherwise, when they come down to the truth, it is the same.

The Conjunction of Atoms is Unreasonable

Obviously what we see is what we see, but our perceptions at a gross level always have some cause behind them. Through investigation and logical analysis we can eventually reach the most subtle state beyond which there is nowhere further to go. Everyone has to agree with this. This is logical. We have to accept something as the foundation of the grosser levels of what we experience. For many people this is known as atoms. This is what every school believes except for the Mahayana and Vajrayana.

According to Buddhist philosophy, this universe, the world and all of these gross things did not exist at the beginning time. It was not like this in the first place. In the beginning there was subtle shifting and moving, transformations back and forth until gradually these gross forms developed. This means that initially the world that we are in was not like it is now. It was completely different from what we see. At some point things began to form. Where did they come from? They came from atoms. These irreducible atoms did not just suddenly become a big chunk of gross things. They were not just hovering around somewhere until they came together. At the beginning there were no heavy gross things anywhere. There was only space. From this space heavy gross things gradually developed through the combination of atoms and molecules, or whatever we call the smallest, fundamental particles that exist.

In Buddhism they say that the subtlest atoms come together with many others to form larger objects the five elements. These atoms represent fire, water, wind, earth and space. Even the finest atoms have the energy of these elements to some degree. Gradually the formation of these elements begins separating according to the levels and parts of the atoms. For example, at some point fire becomes fire. Even though fire is mainly composed of fire atoms it has parts of all of the other types of atoms as well. In Buddhism, this is what the teachings say. These atoms did not exist at the beginning when there was just space so therefore at some point they began to form.

Our discussion deals with the time when these finest, irreducible atoms began to form. We are not talking about gross level objects. It is as if we were sitting on the ground at point zero before forms developed. From there we begin to analyze how things began to form and combine together.

Number one has to come from zero. How will it come about? This is what Vasubandhu is analyzing using logic and reason. Zero and one are very different. Zero means there is actually nothing. One means there is something. From zero how can one develop? How can something arise from nothing? So we are standing at zero and then using these arguments.

Non-Mahayana schools say that there are partless atoms because they have to say something. Everything cannot come from nothingness. There has to be a cause. Therefore they say that partless atoms exist. If partless atoms exist they need to have at least six parts or sides—up, down, north, south, east and west. Even though they are so small they have to have at least six parts. Yet if they have six sides or parts how can they be called 'partless'? If they don't have any parts then they are not really atoms. Every particle must have at least six parts. So the term 'partless atom' doesn't make any sense. If it is truly partless then no matter how many partless particles come together it is not going to make anything. If you add zero to zero it is not going to make any difference. If you add a hundred zeros to one zero it is not going to change anything.

In response to these arguments, non-Mahayana schools such as the Hinayana, and in particular the Kashmiri Vaibhashika school argue that even though partless particles have no parts when many of them come together each of them has a special force that allows them to combine together to make larger entities. This force acts like glue or a magnet. So even though partless particles do not have any parts they can still come together.

Master Vasubandhu replies in the same way as he did before. If these atoms have no parts then it doesn't matter how many come together. It won't change anything. It illogical to think otherwise since there is nothing that could come together in the first place. If all of the atoms are already partless so there are no things that could possibly join together. If you agree that they do not have parts then there are no parts that could come together. One cannot logically accept that partless atoms can join together with other partless atoms. If they did then they would need to have parts.

The Impossibility of Casting a Shadow or Not

Vasubandhu's next argument is that a partless atom cannot produce a shadow. If a partless atom has directional sides then it cannot be partless since it has parts. If it has no parts then it can have no sides. Without any sides it cannot make a shadow. In the morning when sunlight shines from the east does the partless atom produce a shadow to the west or not? If there is no shadow then even if the sun shines from the east it will also shine to the west. Without parts, a partless atom cannot make a shadow however small.

In addition, Vasubandhu demonstrates that partless atoms cannot produce any kind of blockage. Blockage only happens when one part makes contact with another part. Since partless atoms are said to have no parts, they could not block one another in any way. Therefore no matter how many partless atoms you add together they would have to become just one partless atom. Nothing could ever combine together.

Since Vasubandhu's opponent agrees that partless atoms have no parts, then we should not be able to experience any blockage or see any shadows. Everything should be transparent. Since this is not what we experience then logically we cannot agree that partless atoms have no parts. In other words, Vasubandhu uses logic to prove that partless atoms cannot exist.

The Impossibility of Movement, Place or Size

Next, Vasubandhu argues that partless atoms cannot move, be located in space or have a particular size. For example, we may think that we see forms that are blue or yellow, or the shapes of rectangles or squares. We can experience this in an obvious way that we cannot simply ignore. All such things we see are made of atoms, which are made of tiny subatomic particles. What we see has parts. Do the atoms that make up these things have parts or not? In the case of a blue formation, is it made up of one substance or many substances? If many substances are combined together, Vasubandhu has already proven that this cannot happen if the fundamental atoms that make up larger entities do not have parts. And if what you see is just one partless substance then it cannot possibly change. What would change if there were no parts? We cannot logically accept this possibility since it is obvious that what we see does change over time.

If what we see is just one partless substance then gradual progression can never happen. For example, when you walk on this one partless substance, one of two things can happen: either you cannot go anywhere since there is no part for you to move across, or secondly, in any direction you step you are everywhere all at once since this is one partless substance. Similarly, if you take a step on one partless substance there will be no difference between right and left. Stepping right would be the same as stepping left. Or maybe they would not exist at all. In this way, things cannot exist or function if everything is just one partless substance. There would be no divisions such as east and west or north and south.

Different animals such as horses and oxen would not exist. Nothing could exist in different locations. According to normal conceptions we say, "There is a horse. There is an elephant. There is an ox." They can work together or be in separate places. But if everything is in one partless state these categories, divisions and distinctions could not form. Also the physical size of sentient beings would become the same. Small sentient beings that we cannot see and big sentient beings that we see such as elephants—or even bigger—would all be the same size or have no size. There could be no distinctions between big and small.

By investigating and analyzing through logic and reasoning we can demonstrate that partless atoms cannot exist. They cannot be the cause of all the things that we experience. The idea of an irreducible, fundamental particle is just imagination. It is an imputed phenomenon. Even if it was so small that we could not directly perceive it, logically it cannot truly exist.

So why do we continue experiencing things? What is the cause of this? Master Vasubandhu explains that everything is a display of the mind. It is only the mind. He argues that you cannot logically accept the existence of externally existing objects. Everything is mind. As was said before, first Vasubandhu establishes his point through scripture, then through logic, and finally by refuting his opponent's objections. Now we will begin the third section: the refutation of opponents' arguments.

Refuting Objections to the Establishment of Pervasive Certainty by Reasoning

The refutation of the objections of Vasubandhu's opponents has six subdivisions. The first subdivision is that the Mind Only school cannot be hurt by arguments about direct valid cognition. Secondly, the argument that people awake from their dreams cannot refute the Mind Only school's position. Thirdly, the Mind Only school cannot be refuted based on arguments concerning the cause of what is virtuous and what is non-virtuous since virtues and non-virtues do not come from external objects but from the mind. Fourthly, Vasubandhu refutes arguments concerning murdering others since killing arises based on the power of the mind. Fifth, he provides examples that demonstrate how death and murder is based on the power of the mind. Finally, since even reading the minds of others is just a perception arising from one's own mind, this poses no problem for the Mind Only school. These are the six subdivisions known as avoiding the refutations of others.

The First Refutation

The first point is that direct valid cognition cannot hurt the position of the Mind Only school. On the relative level, among all the valid cognitions the supreme valid cognition is direct valid cognition. All inferential valid cognition depends on direct valid cognition. Therefore the root of valid cognition is direct valid cognition.

Opponents of the Mind Only school reply in this way, "If no objects of the senses exist externally, then when you have a direct valid cognition of an object, what do you experience? For example, when the eye consciousness has a direct valid cognition of a form that is true, or if you correctly experience a sound, smell, taste, touch or a feeling with direct valid cognition. How is this possible if everything is mind and external objects do not exist? Does the Mind Only school ignore direct valid cognition?"

The Mind Only school responds that this objection does not disprove its point of view. The experience of all direct valid cognitions is the same as when one is dreaming. Even if you experience something with direct valid cognition it doesn't mean that something solid exists outside of your mind. As in the dream example, one can perfectly experience all objects of the senses even if there are no substantially existing objects outside of the mind.

Vasubandhu says that we have to look closely at what direct valid cognition really means. When the eye organ looks at a form and an eye-consciousness arises, each of these is already changing. The eye organ is changing, forms are changing, consciousness is changing, and thoughts are changing. They are all changing every moment. In one instant there are millions of changes taking place. While the mind registers what you think you saw, what you actually saw has already passed. It is already gone. It has changed and something new has arrived. The moment you think that something is there, it has already left. Even in one instant there are millions and trillions of instances that arise and pass away while you look at something. The senses and mind are always continuously sparking.

Therefore, how can you even talk about direct valid cognition? It's not direct. It is almost always inferred. What you actually see is not exactly what you think you are seeing. This shows that direct valid cognition is already in a very shaky position. Objections based on direct valid cognition cannot disprove or weaken the Mind Only school's view.

When ordinary sentient beings look at an object, the object seems like it is solid and permanently existing. Consciousness seems permanent and solidly existing. The sense organs seem permanently existing and unchanging. This is known as grasping, holding onto permanence. But reality is completely different. This logic applies to everything. For example, on the gross level today is not yesterday. Nor will today be the same as tomorrow. This is the ignorance of sentient beings. They always see similarity and therefore think that everything remains the same all of the time. This is just similar-looking displays of illusion. Otherwise everything is constantly new and different. Things are constantly changing every instant. Even what we would think is just one instant can have hundreds or thousands of instants within it that are continuously changing.

In the Buddha's teaching there is an example which proves that these instants are continuously changing. Let's say there are over two hundred lotus petals stacked up one on top of the other. You put this stack of petals right in front of you on a table. In one hand you hold a sharp needle. The moment you snap the fingers of your other hand you quickly push the needle from the top of the stack all the way down to the bottom of the hundreds of lotus petals. When this needle moves from the top of the stack of petals all the way to the bottom, it pierces each petal in order, one by one. This is a gross example which shows that the moment each petal is individually pierced represents just one of the many instants within the snap of a finger.

Of course there are modern machines that are capable of showing a rapid succession of events in a very short period of time. Actually, these events happen gradually but they occur so quickly that it seems that they all happen at once. Similarly, when we look at something with our eyes, the eye is continually changing. The object and the mind are also both continually changing. Everything exists momentarily. Mind catches something, registers it and then catches something altogether different. It happens so fast that we don't notice the changes taking place. It is moving so fast that it seems like it's the same thing. But actually everything exists only for a very short instant.

The Second Refutation

The second objection raised by opponents of the Mind Only school involves the waking and dreaming of ordinary sentient beings. The objection is that although the Mind Only school often uses dreams as an example to prove its position, everyone knows that dreams are not really real. For, "When we're dreaming, we're dreaming. But then when we wake up there are no more dreams." How can we compare this experience with externally existing things that we actually see while we are awake? When we wake up and the dream disappears, these objects are still here. Therefore, the example of a dream does not prove that external objects do not really exist. And if everything is mind as the Mind Only school claims, out of the billions of people alive at least some regular sentient beings have to realize that everything is a dream—that all of these objects are dreamlike since they don't really exist. But no one says this. Not even one or two people say that these objects don't truly exist since everything is actually a dream. Therefore, you cannot really use this example to support your view that everything is mind. What you are saying is incorrect."

In response, Vasubandhu says that an example one uses while making an argument is not always the same as what one is trying to establish by using the example. If an example and the purpose for using an example are identical then we wouldn't have to use examples. Since there are some distinctions between an example and its purpose, people use examples. In the case of the dream example, everyone agrees that the objects we experience while dreaming are not real. During a dream, the object and the subject do not really exist. Yet while we are dreaming everything seems real. Hundreds of millions of people would agree that while they dream what they experience seems really real. Then when we wake up, it's gone. What seems real while we dream is later shown to be unreal when we wake up. The same is true of our waking experience.

Even if nobody recognizes that what they experience is not real, this does not disprove the view of the Mind Only school. There is hardly anyone who has less grasping and less clinging. Every living being is pretty much the same as long as they are in samsara. They all have nearly the same ways of grasping and clinging. Because of this they are not even going to briefly see that everything is a dream. This is the big dream state of every sentient being caught up in ignorance and duality. Sentient beings are continually grasping and holding onto exaggerations or imputed phenomena. That is why they are obscured. That is why they don't see that the object and subject of their experience do not truly exist externally.

The same thing happens while we are dreaming. Until we wake up, hardly anyone recognizes, "I am dreaming" or "I am not really real." Even in our dreams we do not see this. Yet this doesn't change the fact that the dream is not real. Similarly, we don't see that phenomena exist like a dream or as a display of the mind because we have been deluded by habitual patterns for such a long time, life after life. Our understanding has become spoiled by grasping and clinging. This is the cause of our mistaken understanding. When will these mistakes disappear? When will we see that everything is an illusory display of the mind? This will happen only once we achieve inner wisdom and realization. At that time we will see that everything is a display of the mind. Until then, just using the logic of regular sentient beings concerning examples of dreaming and waking will not hurt the position of the Mind Only school in any way.

The Third Refutation

The third objection raised by non-Mahayana schools is about the Mind Only school's position that virtues and non-virtues do not come from external objects but from the mind. They argue that if everything is a display of the mind then we cannot make distinctions between what is virtuous and non-virtuous. In addition, those in the Mind Only school have contact with virtuous spiritual teachers, receive their teachings and practice virtue. They also avoid non-virtuous teachers and don't follow non-virtuous advice. This shows that the Mind Only school's philosophy cannot be correct. It is contradictory to learn about virtue and non-virtue from beings that exist outside of your mind if everything is mind.

Vasubandhu avoids this refutation by arguing that when you come into contact with qualified teachers and learn about virtue from them, this means that your mind begins to perceive the display of the teacher, and that the mind of the teacher's display also begins to perceive your mind. This is like the echoing back and forth of your mind and its perceptions of the display of your teacher. This is how you learn. The minds of different beings can help one another. This is how the system of interdependence works. Learning means supporting each other by contacting the minds of one another. In addition, virtues are actually ideas, and ideas are nothing other than mind. The power of a virtuous spiritual teacher's mind reflects to your mind and the minds of others. Therefore this objection is not going to weaken the view of the Mind Only school.

Non-virtue functions in the same way. The mind of a non-virtuous teacher or pupil begins to reflect on the surface of the mind of others. As a result, the mind will become adapted to non-virtue, which will develop into habitual patterns. One will then begin to do negative things.

The Fourth Refutation

The next question from the opponents of the Mind Only school again focuses on the dream example: "When someone falls asleep and begins dreaming, at that time one is heavily engaging with the dream world. All external objects that people normally perceive as real become completely useless. They have no basic purpose when one is sleeping. Since the Mind Only school is so occupied with the dream example, it seems that all of these external objects are not important to you. You even say that when we wake up everything we experience is in a dream-like state. You claim that nothing we experience really exists because everything is a dream or a display of the mind. So in a sense you don't make any distinctions between dreaming and the phenomena we experience while we are awake. Yet in a dream if we perform negative activities, they don't produce big consequences. But since dreaming and being awake are the same for the Mind Only school, aren't you saying that there is no difference between doing good and bad activities in the world? Maybe they don't produce any consequences, just like in a dream. If you do virtuous activities, are there no good consequences? If you perform non-virtuous activities don't you receive negative consequences? Therefore, there is not any difference between virtue and non-virtue according to the doctrine of the Mind Only school."

Vasubandhu responds to this objection in the following way. It is true that both dreaming and waking experiences are the display of the mind. Even though both are the display of mind, one involves light habitual patterns and the other involves heavy habitual patterns. Dream experience is based on light habitual patterns therefore they won't hurt oneself or others too much. They don't produce big consequences. But during the daytime the mind is very heavily obscured by dense habitual patterns. Therefore, whatever we do while we are awake has big consequences. So the way the dream-like nature of dreaming and the dream-like nature of the waking state functions is not exactly the same. Therefore we have to follow the systems of what things are good to do and what things are not good to do even if everything is mind. Our actions and their consequences depend on the strength of the habitual patterns that are involved, and habitual patterns come from the mind. They do not come from something that exists externally. Habitual patterns are caused by the power of the mind and the strength and type of one's habitual patterns.

Questions and Answers #4

Question: If the alaya is pervasive and cannot really be accurately described by regular, relative categories such as direction and time, then how can the sixth consciousness, which is the result of the alaya, conceive of past, present and future? What is the cause of this?

Answer: According to all Mahayana schools, conceiving of the past, present and future is grasping. When we go to the department of Dzogchen it says that the three times are led by conceptions. Therefore they speak of original time or the fourth time which is free from the three times. The nature of mind is free from the restrictions of conceptions. The sixth consciousness is grasping which arises as dual consciousness sparking out of the alaya.

Question: Does Vasubandhu believe that this building exists? That it is made out of something outside of the mind?

Answer: Yes, this building appears to exist outside of the mind at present due to habitual patterns. As we discussed before, there are three habitual patterns: habitual patterns of the whole universe, habitual patterns of the objects of the senses, and habitual patterns of the body. Of these three, one includes things that are far away, one includes things at a medium distance, and the body is includes things that are very close. Vasubandhu never ignores these three habitual patterns.

Question: Is it the collective human habitual patterns that cause atoms to appear to form and buildings to be made and so forth?

Answer: In a more general way, habitual patterns can be divided into two different types. One is common habitual patterns and the other is personal, individual habitual patterns. An example of common habitual patterns is that those who are born as human beings all have a similar way of thinking, similar way of seeing, and similar way of proving things. An example of individual habitual patterns is that each of us is part of a family, yet even within that family we all have slightly different ways of perceiving things. Our ideas and opinions can be quite different even though we are all humans.

Common habitual patterns caused this building to be made out of similar materials, with a specific design, the roofing, and all of the ingredients that were necessary to make this building. Yet due to personal habitual patterns different people who come here perceive this building in different ways. Those people who are Buddhist practitioners will see this gonpa as an object of veneration that is beautiful, where they can go and meditate and bring more calm and peace. Others may think that this building is funny looking and that people are doing strange things. Even though we all see the building it appears to us in different ways because we interpret our common habitual patterns according to our individual habitual patterns.

Question: Say a hungry ghost and a human are both standing next to a river. If the human drinks water from the river with his eyes shut will the river water taste like pus?

Answer: No. The human is not a *preta*. Closing one's eyes will not change one's habitual patterns immediately.

Question: So the *preta* will not be able to change what is outside of his mind?

Answer: No, we cannot change what appears to be outside of us so easily. An individual's habitual patterns are very independent in a way. If the habitual patterns could be so easily changed then the Buddha, who is so kind, would have already changed all of our habitual patterns and we would already have become buddhas.

Question: Is it true that tertöns who can put their hands into rocks to pull out termas have broken the three habitual tendencies of world, objects of the senses, and body?

Answer: We don't know if they completely broke through all of the three habitual patterns, but they definitely see that everything is mind. Many tertöns are really very highly enlightened beings, and if not, they're definitely great bodhisattvas. Therefore they have the realization that everything is emptiness and that all appearances are mind. Their dual consciousness is not as strong as the rest of us. That's why they can do things like pulling termas out of solid rock.

Question: I can see how they could break through solidity. But what does it mean that they don't have duality?

Answer: They don't have so much grasping.

Question: What does this have to do with subject and object? Is it that they don't see anything as being different from their own minds?

Answer: They see that object and subject are emptiness. Objects are emptiness. It's like a transparent state of existence. And because of this realization, they can move through what appears to us as solid objects. At present our thought is that rock is so solid and that our hands are different than rock. Our hands are more tender and soft than rock. We have such big distinctions between us and the rock, or any object for that matter. This is due to our grasping and the duality that comes as a result. When you realize that both your hand and rock, or a subject and object both have the same nature of emptiness, then you see that things can always appear from emptiness. Form is emptiness. When you realize that form is emptiness then you also see that emptiness is form. At this point, you see that everything is quite flexible since it is not limited by duality. Therefore so many different things can be performed.

Question: As we work to change the habitual patterns of our own minds, will this change the habitual patterns of the universe?

Answer: If we start changing our own habitual patterns it will definitely help the world's habitual patterns. But the common habitual patterns are not going to change as completely as you changed your habitual patterns. Your share of the habitual patterns will definitely be changed and to some degree this will help others. But their habitual patterns are not going to change exactly as yours did.

Question: Is the mind always carried by a subtle energy?

Answer: Yes.

Question: Then what would the subtle energy be in an enlightened person?

Answer: There are many different varieties of energy. The principle energies are known as love, kindness, compassion, and wisdom. These are really the qualities of the mind or brightness of the mind. When you reach enlightenment these energies fully appear without any of the blockages of the exaggerations or imputed phenomena.

Question: Is that energy based on some kind of material? I mean what is the stuff? Is there any stuff?

Answer: The stuff of these qualities is called non-partiality. These energies are all based on non-grasping.

Question: So there are no elements involved?

Answer: This is true. There are no elements that we can hold. It is called emptiness-mind. It is emptiness. Yet still it appears. Therefore these qualities are made out of what we could call "inconceivable stuff". It is inconceivable, so the duality of this present mind cannot exactly categorize this stuff.

Question: Sometimes I think there is one alaya, and sometimes I think there are two alaya. One is sort of dark, and then the other is something that sparks.

Answer: Generally speaking, there is one alaya. However, even though it is one alaya it has two aspects. The original, true nature of the alaya is very pure and very enlightened. It is sometimes known as absolute alaya or absolute wisdom alaya. The second aspect of the alaya—the surface alaya—is the foundation of habitual patterns, or the storehouse of habitual patterns. So even though there is only one alaya, it has superficial qualities and real qualities.

Question: If the alaya registers things impartially, instead of experiencing things impartially, why do I experience things as either good or bad?

Answer: The alaya is impartial in that it doesn't choose what it registers and what it doesn't register. There's no check post, no border securities and no immigration offices. Whatever comes is allowed to enter. Sometimes good things come and sometimes bad things come. So then good things reflect good and bad things reflect bad.

Question: How did our habitual patterns come about in the first place to cause relative reality? Doesn't there have to be relative reality in order to create habitual patterns?

Answer: In the Buddha's teachings it is often said that the beginning of the habitual patterns was caused by grasping and clinging.

Question: But what did we grasp onto? Who was originally clinging?

Answer: We clung to the ripples of the alaya. We clung onto one ripple of the alaya's waves and that was the beginning of the habit of grasping. Why were we grasping? It is often said that we didn't have awareness. We didn't recognize that the ocean of the alaya and its waves are inseparable.

Question: So this is where beginningless time comes in?

Answer: Yes, that's the beginning of beginningless time. In the West they say that's the beginning of the chicken and the egg.

Question: Can you tell us the relationship between alaya and Tathagatagarbha?

Answer: Pure alaya is also named tathagatagarbha. The tathagatagarbha is wisdom or nature of the dharmadhatu. But if it is blocked by exaggeration it cannot be fully expressed. However, the seed or potential is always there.

Question: This means that in addition to our habitual patterns, intrinsic wakefulness is also sparkling through.

Answer: That's it.

Question: That's good news.

Answer: That's what they call the light at the end of the tunnel. This is our light at the end of the tunnel. It is the Good Morning News.

The Fourth Refutation Continued

And now we return to the text itself. We continue where we left off before. In the main section of the *Twenty Verses* Vasubandhu presents six different statements that refute the objections of others. Of these six, we are on the fourth refutation. This corresponds to the 19th or the 20th stanza.

Here Vasubandhu explains that death and murder is a result of the power of the mind. Opponents of the Mind Only school raise the objection that if everything is mind, then what happens when a person kills someone else—or when any type of being kills another being? If everything is mind then why does a killer have obscurations as a result of the murder he or she commits? If it is really just mind, it is not actually killing. It is just your mind. And since you argue that everything is mind, in a way you are rejecting the existence of body and speech. If you only accept the existence of mind, then murder could not happen because no one exists apart from the mind. Therefore mind cannot kill anyone and it cannot be killed by someone. So why do you say that a killer has obscurations or that murder and death are even possible?

Master Vasubandhu responds to this objection by saying that even though everything is a habitual pattern of the mind, there are light habitual patterns and there are heavy habitual patterns. Our body and speech are determined by heavy habitual patterns. Even though deep down everything is mind, on the surface there are dense habitual patterns of clinging onto body and speech. Therefore even though everything is mind, when you hurt or kill someone your mind is disturbing the existing habitual patterns of the other person's mind.

And what is death, actually? Death is the changing of a situation. It is a transition between different states. It is a big change when death comes. Generally speaking, consciousness continues uninterruptedly. When a big change appears in consciousness—this is known as death.

What is life about? Life is warmth, breath and consciousness. When warmth, breathing, and consciousness co-exist together it is called life.

These three factors are also just habitual patterns. When you interrupt the existing habitual patterns of others' warmth, breath and consciousness, the power of your mind affects the power of someone else's mind. The result of this is karma. Karma is the obscurations of one's mind. Therefore generally speaking, murder, life and death are all powers of the mind, and mind can have obscurations, fabrications and karma.

The Fifth Refutation

Here master Vasubandhu uses an example that was widely accepted in India, Tibet and Asia during his lifetime and is still accepted today. It is a common belief that when people have a lot of psychological problems and their mind becomes really unbalanced, the cause could be some type of invisible being. There might be other causes as well, but it is also possible that invisible beings could be deluding someone's mind. In the West there are also some people who believe that demons and gods exist and that they can influence people's minds. In order for these beliefs to still be current nowadays some of our great ancestors must have believed in them as well. Vasubandhu uses this widely accepted belief as an example to prove his point. When demons influence and obscure someone's mind, it is the power of their mind that influences the power of another being's mind. This too is only the power of the mind. Then the power of the mind influences our physical actions.

When people go into a trance, it is caused by the power of the mind. Channelling is also the power of the mind. Sometimes people say that they have good dreams that actually happen and bad dreams that actually happen. They also talk about having dreams that actually happen, only a long time afterwards. Some people are not just saying these things—they actually experience them. When people say that they receive the blessings of Guru Padmasambhava and of all the Buddhas—this is also the power of the mind. Recently many scientists have proved that when people pray it works. I saw this on television but I don't know exactly if it is true. Nevertheless, it is common for people to ask others to pray for them. This also is an effect of the mind. It is not an effect of anything physical. This shows that everyone agrees, whether they admit it openly or not, that the mind works.

And there are also stories that demonstrate the power of mind. In ancient times, when Buddha was in India he had many thousands of disciples. Among them there was one named the noble disciple Katayana. Katayana was one of the Buddha's very famous disciples. Often Buddha honored him saying that he had the power to benefit others where there was no Dharma. He could travel to the far edge of the country and teach Dharma. This would really help the people there. He was one of the supreme arhats who could help the beings who lived in places where no buddhas or other arhats had gone or taught before.

Once, Katyayana planned to go to a place where the Dharma had never been taught. In this place lived a man named Sarana. Sarana had never heard the Dharma and he was a very wild, tough man. He was a regular guy with no interest in spiritual things or the Dharma. Through his wisdom mind, Katyayana saw that Sarana was ready to enter the Dharma. He also saw that if Sarana entered the Dharma he would be able to inspire many beings on the path of enlightenment. In order to do this, Katyayana meditated and through the power of his mind, he directed blessings towards Sarana. That night Sarana had elaborate dreams about Katayana coming to his town and helping, guiding and supporting the people there. In his dream, Sarana felt very happy and relaxed. He then woke up with a very beautiful and fresh recollection of this dream. Then soon after that Katayana arrived. When Sarana saw Katayana, he almost fainted. What he saw in the dream and what he saw now with his eyes were the same. Katyayana then did activities and gave teachings in the exact same way that he did in Sarana's dream. For Sarana, meeting Katyayana was like meeting someone again that he had already met in his dream. Immediately Sarana opened his heart and he entered the Dharma. This was made possible by the power of Katayana's mind or his blessings.

There is another story from ancient pre-Buddhist history. In ancient times the gods and asuras were always fighting. Buddha taught about this as well. During this time there was there was a very famous and powerful rishi named Rishi Gonpa. Rishi Gonpa could do whatever he liked because his mind was highly achieved. At that time the king of the asuras was Tazangri. Tazangri came to this Rishi Gonpa and offered him to help him anytime he needed it. Rishi Gonpa accepted his offer and became the teacher of King Tazangri. Rishi Gompa always supported the king, and as a result, when the gods and asuras fought the asuras would always win. This was possible because of the power of Rishi Gompa's mind. Sometime later, when Tazangri continued to win battles he became arrogant and disrespectful to rishi Gonpa. He also began to misuse his power by hurting and disturbing many beings. When this happened Rishi Gonpa became upset. He immediately said, "May Tazangri not win his battles with the gods." The moment he said this immediately Tazangri began losing his battle with the gods. During ancient times this was a widely believed story. Master Vasubandhu uses this example to show that everything is the power of the mind.

Simply put, Vasubandhu is saying is that until we are free from duality we will be stuck within the innumerable systems of duality. This is true even though everything is mind. All good and bad things will seem to exist to us even though they are mind. Therefore we have to do good things and avoid bad things. The moment we wake up and finish all duality, we will reach the original state of the true nature of the alaya. At that time everything will be completely different. But until then we have to be very careful with our deeds of body, speech and mind. Even though everything is mind we should not ignore even the tiniest deed that we perform.

Vasubandhu uses another example to refute the fifth objection from non-Mahayana opponents of the Mind Only school. The power of the mind can hurt others. Generally, in all of the Buddha's teaching, from the Hinayana through the Mahayana, Buddha always said that mind is the principal thing. Mind is like a king or queen, and body and speech are like assistants. Buddha taught this in the Hinayana teachings as well. He said that mind is quick. Mind always occurs before an action. Every action we do and whatever we see, mind always comes before the action.

Again, we're not saying that the Buddha said that it *should* be this way. When we think carefully we will see that this is true. Everything we do is accompanied by the mind. Mind always occurs a few seconds before our actions. For example, we are gathered here because mind. You thought that you would like to listen to this teaching. After you had that thought the actions and activities which followed caused us to all gather here today. For this reason the Buddha always emphasized the fact that mind is very important because it is the principal factor of all actions, and that therefore we should always be mindful, alert, attentive and modest. All of these teachings are mainly teachings on how the mind functions and on how the mind has to act in order to achieve peace and happiness for oneself and for others.

We are always talking about these things. We always talk about good things that we all love such as love, kindness, compassion, honesty and truth. All of these are really no other than mind. We talk about the mind using different terms that refer to the way the mind's qualities reflect externally even though they are inherent qualities of the mind. This is why we use different names. But deep down all of these good qualities are really no other than mind.

Because of all that, we have to always be careful with the mind. We have to always watch our mind and be mindful of our speech and our actions. In Buddha's teaching this is acknowledged as the most powerful practice. For this reason, the great master Shantideva taught in his *Bodhisattvacharyavatara* that there is no other ascetic practice than to watch your mind. If you watch your mind, remaining mindful from moment to moment, then every ascetic practice is accomplished.

Therefore, he said, "With folded hands I request that all of you watch your mind."

Here master Vasubandhu introduces a story that actually happened during the time of the Buddha. Buddha Shakyamuni met with a householder named Newakor in Tibetan or Upali in Sanskrit. The Buddha asked him if he knew what had happened to the villages of Dentaka, Kalingka, and Matangka. "These three villages have completely disappeared", he said, "Do you know what happened? What do people say about this?"

Newakor told the Buddha that because of a powerful curse from a rishi the villages of Dentaka, Kalingka and Matangka have disappeared. That's what Newakor heard people say.

The Buddha told Newakor that that was true. The power of a rishi's curse was capable of destroying all of those villages. The mind is so powerful. Because of the power of the mind whatever the mind does produces a result that is also very heavy.

The root of a curse is negative intention. Many people believe that if somebody has a bad intention and curses them, soon after they have different kinds of trouble, the cause of which is the curse. That's what people sometimes say.

Deep down this is caused by the power of the mind. The power of the mind is capable of manipulating and controlling a situation. We can experience this. The power of the mind comes from the strength of one's concentration. If we have strong, good concentration then the power of the mind becomes very strong. That is why it is said that rishis have great powers of concentration. In Tibetan, rishis are called *drang song*. One becomes a *drang song* by always keeping the mind and body—particularly the mind—focused in one direction all the time. Such a person does not perform any negative activities and does not let the mind carelessly fall into regular habitual patterns. By continually maintaining one state of mind all of the time, a person can develop the power of concentration. By making the mind stay continually in a single state that is virtuous, one becomes capable of doing powerful things that are virtuous.

Of course the power of the Buddha, the power of the Dharma and the power of the Sangha is often said to be even greater when they are united together and maintained in a single state of awareness. The results are really quite amazing. They are even more powerful.

The Sixth Refutation

The sixth objection that Vasubandhu refutes pertains to how people can see or read other people's minds. This is an instance of a mind perceiving another mind.

Again, the opponent of the Mind Only school makes an objection: "If everything is mind then are you going to agree that mind can see mind? Or that mind can see the mind of others? If people cannot see the mind of others, then we can say that they can't see the mind of others. If people can see the mind of others, then how can they see it? Do they see the mind of others exactly as it is or not exactly as it is?

Vasubandhu replies to this objection by using the second option: the mind can see the mind of others. But when mind sees the mind of others it doesn't happen in exactly the same way that an eye sees forms. It's not exactly this way because mind cannot see the complete image of the mind of others as the eye can see the complete image of forms. So what does the mind see if it doesn't see another's mind in exactly the same way as an eye sees forms? If someone has the capabilities, their mind can see the grasping in the mind of others as well as the waves and currents of thoughts that are arising in someone else's mind. That aspect of mind it can really see. And when one sees this it is said that the mind can see or read the mind of others. Of course we can read our own mind. But even when we truly look at our own mind to see how it is we cannot see exactly how it is because mind is inconceivable and inexpressible. We cannot fully and exactly read our mind even by ourselves. However, we can see for ourselves the formations of the currents of ideas and conceptions in our mind. In this way, we can truthfully say that we can read our own mind.

This is the last point of the six points that Vasubandhu refutes in the section called "refuting the objections of others."

The Benefits of the Teaching of the Mind Only School

The last section in the main body of this teaching addresses what the benefits are of holding the Mind Only school position that everything is mind. What is the benefit of this?

The benefit of this is that when you begin to see that everything is mind and the display of the mind, you will begin to discover the true nature of every phenomenal system. You will begin to discover what the truth is. If you truly begin to actualize this view, you also won't be completely tormented by the suffering of dualistic activities of mind and body. You will see that everything appears as a result of one's own mind. All the things that make us suffer and feel happy are nothing other than our own mind. Therefore the smart and wise ones will reduce and eventually eliminate dualistic activity. This will cause them to gradually be freed from the cyclic existence of habitual patterns.

Vasubandhu then says that he presented the teachings of the Mind Only school according to the capabilities of his realization. Ultimate realization of the Mind Only school is something that even he cannot explain. The teaching of the Mind Only school cannot be fully explained exactly as it is by the conceptual mind. Ideas and concepts cannot reach the depths of the Mind Only school since it is so profound. It can only be discovered by the Buddha's enlightened mind.

The teaching of the Mind Only school is the essential, ultimate teaching of the Buddha. Therefore if you discover the view and the philosophy of the Mind Only school, you are discovering true nature as it is. Because of this we can reach enlightenment and benefit all living beings. This is the reason that Vasubandhu explained the teachings of the Mind Only school.

Generally all the teachings of Buddhism talk about the mind. Mind is so important. Again this is not only what Buddha said. It is not just something that we believe in. This is not really the case in Buddhism. It is something into which you must look using your own knowledge and your own wisdom. If it suits you then you should accept it. If it doesn't suit you then you should make a serious inquiry and find out the facts of the matter.

These teachings come from so many great intellectuals—the champions of the intellectuals. The champions of thinkers thought about these questions and thoroughly examined them. They dissected these problems in so many different ways using intellectual tools and meditation, and found these teachings as the result. So these issues have already been investigated and analyzed. They have already been put through the process of logical inquiry and the result is here. Therefore it is very accurate. It corresponds with how natural phenomena function and with the way that all things communicate according to subject and object. Yet it is still not something that we have to blindly believe in. We can examine and analyze this for ourselves.

When we actually perform this investigation we realize that everything comes down to the mind. Mind is the most important, principal thing. Every school and philosophical doctrine of Buddhism says that mind is principal. In a way, the Vaibhashika school is the only school that reduces the importance of mind. For example, the Vaibhashika school asserts that when an eye sees a form, a substantial eye-consciousness goes and catches a substantial object of the form. They believe in the substantial existence of both subject and object. That's why they can catch one another. This process is called seeing. The Vaibhashika school explains the communication between all the senses and their objects in this same way. Yet in the *Abhidharmakosha* even the Vaibhashika school agrees that this universe and all of samsara comes from karma. And where does karma come from? Karma comes from the mind. In this way we can see that even the Vaibhashika school emphasizes the importance of the mind.

The views from the Sautrantika school all the way to Dzogchen openly agree that everything is mind. In the Mind Only school we discover that everything is mind. In the Madhyamaka—e.g. in Svatantrika Madhyamaka—the great master Shantarakshita also says that everything is mind. According to the relative truth of our perception, everything is no other than the mind. He established this conclusion through logic and reasoning. Above the Svatantrika Madhyamaka is the Prasangika Madhyamaka or *Thalgyurwa (thal 'gyur ba)*. In the *Thalgyurwa* the great master Chandrakirti said that everything in this universe is composed or reflected by karma. Karma is made by the mind. If you release the mind there is no karma and no obscurations. This causes you to reach to the Great Emptiness, the ultimately true nature.

In the practices of outer tantra, visualization of the deity with a mantra circling in the heart center, the recognition that there is nothing else besides the sound aspect of the mind, and everything else—all of the principal practices of each level of outer tantra are based on the realization that everything is mind.

In the inner tantras—Mahayoga, Anuyoga and Atiyoga tantras—seeing the three mandalas and the union of the Great Equanimity pure from the beginning are all based on discovering the nature of mental states. In the Mind section (*Semde*) of Dzogchen it is often said that you begin to see everything as mind. Everything is seen as the display of the mind. One discovers that mind is already free in the state of Great Emptiness.

From the Mind Only all the way through to Dzogchen, everything is a display of the mind. And mind is pure from the beginning *(ka dag)*. It is for this reason that Vasubandhu said that the Mind Only teaching is so profound. Vasubandhu said that even he did not know their full meaning since only the enlightenment of a Buddha can fully discover the complete meaning of the Mind Only school teachings. We are touching to the reality of ultimate nature from here all the way to Dzogchen.

Conclusion

We have now arrived at the fourth section of the *Twenty Verses*. The last section is the conclusion. The conclusion states that the *Twenty Verses* composed by Vasubandhu are completed. Who translated Vasubandhu's original text into Tibetan? During the mid-eighth century three great Indian masters translated the *Twenty Verses*. Their names were Jinamitra, Jalendrabodhi, and Danashila. These three Indian masters worked under the guidance of the chief translator and editor Bhande Yeshe De, who also translated this text into Tibetan, corrected it, recorrected it, and then reconfirmed the accuracy of this text once it was translated into Tibetan.

Mipham Rinpoche's Commentary

And what is the story behind Mipham Rinpoche's commentary on the *Twenty Verses*? When Mipham Rinpoche passed away, one of his great disciples went through all of his manuscripts and found Mipham Rinpoche's footnotes to the *Twenty Verses*. The disciple's name was Shechen Gyaltsap of Shechen Monastery. Shechen Gyaltsap rewrote these footnotes in exactly the same way that Mipham Rinpoche had written them and he published them. At the end of Mipham Rinpoche's commentary Shechen Gyaltsap himself writes: "These footnotes were written by the omniscient Mipham, who followed the auto-commentary of the Second Buddha Vasubandhu exactly. I, Shechen Gyaltsap, transcribed these footnotes at the hermitage of Shechen Monastery."

This completes the brief teachings on the *Twenty Stanzas*.

Longchenpa's Wish-Fulfilling Treasure

This is our brief talk on the Mind Only school. However, these teachings are very profound and therefore we will now go to the great master Longchenpa's writings which put together the whole picture of the conduct and achievement of the Mind Only school. Longchenpa wrote many different teachings which are now known as the teachings of the *Seven Treasures*. Many of the Seven Treasures focus on the views of the Mind Only school. One of the teachings is called the *Wish-Fulfilling Treasure* of Longchenpa, and it has a section on the different Buddhist and non- Buddhist doctrines called, in Tibetan, *Yizhin Dzo Kyi Drupta (yid bzhin mdzod kyi grub mtha')*. Last year we spoke about the Vaibhashika and the Sautrantika schools according to Longchenpa's *Yizhin Dzo Kyi Drupta* as summarized by Mipham Rinpoche.

The Mind Only school has two major subdivisions. The first subdivision is called *semtsam namdenpa (sems tsam rnam bden pa)*. *Nam* means aspect. *Den* is truth. Altogether this can be translated as the "true aspect of the mind" or "the true image or picture of the mind." The second subdivision is *semtsam namdzunpa (sen tsam rnam rzun pa)*. Again, *nam* means aspect. *Dzun* is different or false. So this is called the "false aspect of the mind" or "the incorrect picture or image of the mind." These are really rough translations.

The true aspect of the mind sub-school of the Mind Only has three more sub-schools. The first is named *zung zin drang nyam pa (gzung 'dzin grangs mnyam pa)*. The second subschool is *go nga che tsal pa (sgo nga phyed tshal pa)*. The third subdivision is *na tsog nyi me pa (sna tshogs gnyis med pa)*. These are the three subdivisions of the true aspect of the mind sub-school of the Mind Only school.

What is the meaning of the first subschool, *zung zin drang nyam pa*? Zung means "object." Dzin means "subject." So object and subject. And *drang* is "numbers." Nyam means "equal." So that means equally numbers of subject and object. So the number of the subject and object is equal. What does this mean actually? For example, when the eye looks at this wall, the wall has so many colors—so many stripes and so many shapes. It has a variety of things. However many objects or images are seen, that same number of consciousnesses are going to "catch" these objects. This means that there is an equal number of objects perceived and subjects that perceive. So the numbers of subjects and objects are equal. That is why we are able to see perfectly. According to this sub-school, all of our sense consciousnesses work in this same way.

There are only slight differences between the other subdivisions. The second sub-school says that the subject and objects seem to be independent on the surface level. That is why this sub-school is called *go nga tsal pa. Go nga* means egg. If you take a boiled egg and cut it in half the yellow part and the white part remain exactly as they are. They stay completely and exactly separated as two things although together they make up one egg. Similarly, in the case of seeing a form, the subject (i.e., one's consciousness) and the object (e.g., an apple) seem to merge although really there are two separate parts: there is an object part and a subject part. In a way, they seem to exist independently according to a surface level of investigation, yet they are both necessary for all of the sense consciousnesses to function correctly.

The third division of the true aspect of mind sub-school of the Mind Only school says something but a little different. This time it is true that the subject and object seem to be different, but when it comes to the subjective, mental aspect of one's experience everything comes together. There are not really many differences at all. All experiences come together in one single state of mind because everything merges in a single instantaneous state. Therefore this sub-school is named *na tsog nyi med pa. Na tsog* means variety. Even if you look externally and you begin to see a variety of appearances -so many colorful things- when it comes to the mind all of them merge together as one in a single instant of mind.

These are the three subdivisions of the true aspect of mind school of the Mind Only school.

The fourth sub-division of Mind Only is *nam zunpa*. While *nam denpa* means true aspect, *nam dzunpa* means false aspect. This means that whatever you see in the mind or whatever the senses perceive is only just an image. It is false. Therefore it is called the false aspect school of the Mind Only school.

There are many more things to say but for now we will keep it simple.

Questions and Answers #5

Question: My question is about the second sub-school, *go nga tshal pa*. What is meant by the subject and object existing equally or *independently*? If the object exists apart from the subject then couldn't it exist apart from this mind?

Answer: This is definitely a very good question. At first it looks as though the object could exist apart from the subject, which is mind. However, here the Mind Only school is talking in a very subtle way. It means that the appearance of the subject and the appearance of the object are independent. There is one mental state whose two aspects appear as being separate. One aspect appears as a subject and the other appears as an object. Both are the mind. The appearance of an object is what you perceive. This is mind. The subject is what you think, which is also mind. But when it comes to the mind, it is said that there are two different aspects that seem to be distinct from one another.
Question: And this is where we have the ignorance of duality?

Answer: Yes, it is duality. *Zung nam* (*gzung rnam*) is the object of the appearance and d*zin nam* (*'dzin rnam*) is the subject of the appearance. Nam is a Tibetan word that means "aspect." *Nam* is the appearance or the image.

Let's look at the example of perception. Perception itself is divided into subject and object. When you look at an object you see an image. This image aspect of seeing is also mind. This is known as *zung nam*.

Immediately after this image appears the mind usually labels the image in some way. It knows or understands something about the image. Who knows something about this image? It is no other than the mind. The subjective understanding is an aspect of mind called *dzin nam*. It is very subtle and happens very quickly.

We can connect this with the previous example of sticking a pin through a stack of lotus petals in the snap of a finger. This happens almost instantly. The mind projects an object which it perceives. The first instant mind perceives. This aspect of the mind is called "the object aspect." The next instant the mind kind of confirms whatever it is that it perceives. This second instant is known as "the subject aspect." The subject and object aspects occur in sequence in two different instants. This is why for this school, even though everything is mind, these two aspects of mind appear to exist separately like when you cut a hard-boiled egg in half. It's a very subtle process.

Question: So first we perceive an object. This object is really our mind but we don't recognize that it is our mind. We immediately think that it is something apart from us. So even in this first instant, we perceive the object because of distortion or ignorance. We are not seeing the object in pure vision. In other words, everything that we perceive is distorted. So even though I see this wall, for example, what I'm seeing is not really what I am seeing.

Answer: Yes, that's true. There is a very famous Nyingma master, Khenpo *Ngakchung*. He said that according to Dzogchen, when you are meditating, relaxing your mind in the one instant state or the original state—at that time the subject, grasping aspect of mind is dissolved. But still, the object aspect of mind remains because we still see things. But when you look inwardly, you recognize that the grasping aspect of mind is dissolved. Of course this is more related with meditation than studying. But when this happens you will understand what subject and object really means. When we're meditating, if we are really in the original status of *Trekchö*, we don't have any kind of categories of thought that arise due to analysis. So at this time the *dzin nam* is dissolved. But of course during this time we will still see things. The *zung nam* still exists.

Another way to understand this is when you look at us and you think that you see us. What you see is an image of us. It looks like us. For you, this image is an object. So you see the image of an object that you saw. When you see this image—that is actually your mind, the object aspect of the mind. And then in the second moment when you confirm what this image is—this is just the mind labelling its projection. It is your mind identifying itself though it doesn't realize that this object is an aspect of itself. This is the subject aspect of the mental consciousness. This is why everything is said to be mind. All of this is mind and the perceptions of the mind.

Question: According to Dharmakirti, the meditator-type of direct valid cognition is inconceivable to the other three types of direct valid cognition. How does the meditator-type of direct valid cognition relate to those other three? If you have the meditator direct valid cognition do you automatically have the other ones? Or do you have part of them? How do they function together?

Answer: They are connected. All four types of direct valid cognition are really connected to one another. The yogi or the yogini's direct valid cognition actually has all four of them together. A yogini can have all four types of direct valid cognition completely. Of course, this depends on the realization of the yogi or yogini. But they can have this. People who don't have yogic power have all of the three other types of direct valid cognition.

Question: Does this mean that a meditator with a certain level of yogic direct valid cognition would automatically have all of this informational knowledge, like where such-and-such place is in the world or how to fix a car when it is broken? Would this automatically happen if you only worked with meditator type of direct valid cognition, or would you have to study and learn these things according to the other types of direct valid cognition?

Answer: Yes, this can definitely happen. The power of a yogi's realization can definitely expand their knowledge. For example, at the first bhumi or even on the first path of accumulation, the direct valid cognition of the meditator depends on your realization within that particular path. If your realization increases more and more, higher and higher, then on the six, seventh and tenth bhumis, one's knowledge really expands. So according Buddhism, the answer is yes. Even if you haven't learned how to fix a car when it is broken, with enough direct valid cognition of meditation your knowledge will naturally expand and you will know how to fix it.

Question: If I understood what you said about inferential valid cognition, it is the type of cognition that we humans mainly have. We can't actually know certain things because of the limitations of space and time. But it would seem that Buddhas who are omniscient would have 100% direct valid cognition. They don't have to infer anything. Is this correct?

Answer: In Buddhism, this is really true. A Buddha has no need for this inferential valid cognition because everything is direct valid cognition. A buddha is always fully in the state of direct valid cognition. We have to use inferential valid cognition because we do not know something directly. For us, everything is not direct valid cognition. Therefore, we often have to use the approach of inferred valid cognition.

Question: Would a good working definition of attaining realization be when a being infers less and less, and directly cognizes more and more?

Answer: Yes, that's really true according to the teaching. The second bhumi's direct valid cognition is much stronger, deeper and broader than the first bhumi. This continues up through the bhumis. On the tenth bhumi almost everything is known by direct valid cognition. For this reason, in a prayer to Manjushri—who is a buddha (even when he appears as a bodhisattva) and therefore always knows according to direct valid cognition—it says: "Pure from the beginning, perfect with the qualities of the ten bhumis, principal son of the Victorious Ones, I pay homage to you." When you have the great wisdoms everything is in the state of direct valid cognition status. Therefore we praise and pay homage to such beings.

Question: The dharmakaya level is absolute reality. And there is a Dharmakaya Buddha. So does Buddha know everything because Buddha is everything?

Answer: In one way this is true. It is said that every aspect of phenomenal objects is equally perfected in the pure state of the nature. When you discover the pure state of the nature as it is, then every phenomenal object is recognized as the arising energy or the arising image or formation of that nature. You discover everything as it is. Every aspect of phenomenal existence is the arising energy or reflection or display of the nature. When you see that everything is completed within that one single natural state—when you see everything as it is—then you will also see all of the images, reflections and displays clearly. This is sometimes called the wisdom of Dharmakaya.

Question: Say somebody gets over their habits by purifying their alaya. Then this person won't have any habitual patterns. In this case, even though an object like a bowl may be visible to everyone else who still has certain habitual patterns, will this person see the bowl?

Answer: When a being's habitual patterns are totally dissolved and finally gone he or she is known as a buddha or a great bodhisattva. Yet at that time, it is not true that all of this will disappear. Everything will become like a display. It will be in a transparent, lucid state. When you reach Buddhahood it doesn't mean that all of this is gone. Everything can exist exactly as it is but without being solid and concrete, filled with all types of divisions. Instead, everything will appear as a magical display. It is said in the teachings that when you have this realization you will see that even within one atom millions of universes can exist. Millions of eons exist within one instant. It is said that at that time the eons have not become shorter and the instants have not become longer. This is known as the realization of equanimity.

The mind of duality cannot really penetrate this and cannot maintain this depth of realization. For this reason Vasubandhu said that only the Buddha can know the inconceivable nature of the Mind Only school. Vasubandhu said that even he did not know the Mind Only school entirely. This is how everything is flexible or in a state of total openness.

Question: When Tara sees Manjushri, they see each other as a display. They know that everything that appears is merely an appearance. It is all empty of substantial existence. But can still see each other as a display and still interact?

Answer: Yes. This is really true. They can see each other. They can talk to each other. They can visit each other. Really, I'm not joking. This is in the Buddha's teachings. They can go to different places like different pure lands, chit chat, and come back in the evening. They can perform every function that sentient beings do.

Question: So they're just constantly without any breakage in their understanding that there is no difference between themselves and others?

Answer: Yes. Even though they are visiting each other and chit chatting, they don't have to go through hope and fear, doubt and dissatisfaction, and feelings of being uncomfortable. They don't have any of these thoughts or attitudes at all. Everything is clear and brilliant. They enjoy the beauty of the nature.

Question: An enlightened being sees an object as a display. But for him where do objects come from? Where is the display coming from? Do the habitual patterns of sentient beings cause him to see these objects as a display? I still don't understand why such a being would he see any objects at all.

Answer: In general, the Buddha has two things. First, the Buddha has what is known as absolute pure alaya. For a buddha, the habitual alaya is transformed into the absolute alaya. All the kayas and all the wisdom displays of the Buddhas of which we are talking about—like them enjoying one another, meeting and chit chatting—all of this is really the display of the absolute alaya. The nature of a particular object and the nature of all displays the Buddha recognizes as Great Emptiness or Great Equanimity; as dharmakaya or the dharmadhatu state. At the same time, a buddha sees what sentient beings see. Because of the power of his wisdom, a buddha can see exactly how sentient beings perceive forms and qualities. Therefore it is said that the Buddha's wisdom expresses itself according to the knowledge of each sentient being. The Buddha perceives the knowledge of every sentient being exactly. Yet the Buddha also has his or her own knowledge. So in a way there are two aspects of wisdom.

These two wisdoms are known as *ji tawe yeshe* and *ji nye pe yeshe. Ji tawe yeshe* is wisdom that knows the nature exactly as it is. It knows emptiness as it is. The second type of wisdom, *ji nye pe yeshe*, knows the variety of aspects and displays of relative truth exactly as they are. It knows everything exactly as it is, whatever it is. This type of wisdom is mentioned in a prayer of Manjushri. Part of the prayer reads: "Seeing all the variety of objects just as they are..." This is *ji nye pe yeshe*. These are the two wisdoms of a buddha.

Question: We say that we will work for the benefit of all beings until all of them become enlightened and samsara is emptied. When samsara is emptied it doesn't necessarily mean that the form realm dissolves and disappears entirely. Does it mean then that when all beings are enlightened, all of the beings that exist in the form realm are seen as nirmanakaya buddhas but the form realm still exists?

Answer: We vow to work for all the sentient beings until samsara is finished. We work for this. But what does this actually mean? It doesn't mean that form is going to disappear or that the desire realm will become completely finished and then vanish. It means that we are going to work until the dualities of all beings are gone. That's the real meaning. That's it. When duality is gone, beings can take any form. They can be human beings. They can be animals. They can be material forms if they like to. Duality is samsara. Samsara is duality. Bodhisattvas continue working until the nature of duality is recognized and samsara comes to an end.

Summary

Among the four schools or doctrines of Buddhism, last year we discussed the first two: Vaibhashika and Sautrantika. This year we began discussing the Mahayana schools. We already covered the seven different qualities that demonstrate why Mahayana is considered to be the "Great Vehicle." Mahayana can be divided into two groups: the Mind Only school and the Madhyamaka schools. Among these two schools we have been investigating the Mind Only school, which was mainly revealed and rekindled by the great master Vasubandhu according to one of his teachings known as the *Twenty Stanzas*.

We will now summarize the Mind Only school according to the teachings of the great master Longchenpa. The entire range of the Mind Only school can be divided into three categories. These are sometimes called the "Three Characteristics" or the "Three Natures." The Three Natures can be understood as the general framework which includes all of the teachings of the Mind Only school.

The first category within the Three Natures framework is imputed or labelled phenomena (*kuntag*). We can roughly translate this as "exaggeration." The second category is the "Powers of Others" or the "Power of the Other Phenomena", e.g., dependent phenomena. The final category is the "Fully Established", "Truly Existing" or the "Establishment of the Final Fact." These are just rough translations of the three characteristics or the three natures. Now we will go into more details.

Imputed Phenomena

The Mind Only school is a very sophisticated and profound philosophical system. The first category of the Mind Only school—exaggeration or imputed phenomena—can be divided into two sections: the first is *tsen nyid che pai kun tag* (*mtshan nyid chad pai kun btags*). The second division is *nam drang pe kun tag* (*rnam grangs pa'i kun btags*). These are the divisions of imputed-labelled phenomena.

Exaggeration Without Characteristics

"*Tsen nyid*" means characteristics. "*Che pe*" means freed or absence. Together this is roughly translated as the "imputation of the absence of characteristics" or "imputation that is without characteristics." So what is this? An example of an imputation that has no characteristics is ego-clinging or clinging onto the self and others. Clinging onto the self and onto others only exists on the relative level. Ultimately, neither the self nor others exist in any way whatsoever. It is only because we label it that it seems to have characteristics. Mind makes labels about something that isn't even there. There is not any real, substantially existing entity like a bowl or a mountain. These are completely the mind's creation. The mind creates ideas about these entities and then we continue holding onto these ideas. This is why it is called the Absence of the Characteristics. It is the imputation of something that never existed at all. The characteristics that seem to appear are completely imaginary. In regard to this type of imputation, if you carefully use logic and reason you will never find any characteristics that actually exist.

Dependently Nominated Entities

The second section of imputed phenomena is *nam drang pa*. *Nam dren pa* literally means "countable" or "able to be numbered." This section is roughly translated as "countable imputations" or "dependently nominated things." These entities do not independently exist as external objects. Due to different situations we name one thing after another, like right and left, this and that, high and low. Dependently nominated things include everything that is labelled in this way. It even includes things like when you look at the moon and press your eye with your finger and you see two moons. Or say you have an eye problem and begin to see double images. Another example is if you take drugs and experience various types of hallucinations. The hallucinations are based on your normal awareness but the drugs distort and exaggerate your perceptions. It is almost as if you see a duplication of what is already exists. In general, whenever you name an object that exists relatively you will automatically label its opposite. All of these types of perceptions are called countable exaggerations or variety exaggerations.

Dependent Phenomena

The second category of the Mind Only school is the "Other-Powered Phenomena" or "Dependent Phenomena" *(zhen wang)*. Dependent phenomena are the source of the two types of imputed phenomena. Deep down, dependent phenomena are the eighth consciousness. The eighth consciousness is the power of others. Due to the power of the eighth consciousness we begin to perceive and experience the limitless variety of different things. Dependent phenomena can also be further divided into two groups. They are called the "impure dependent phenomena" and the "pure dependent phenomena."

Impure Dependent Phenomena

Impure dependent phenomena are the eighth consciousness combined with grasping, clinging, or ignorance. Due to these afflictions, whatever we begin to perceive and experience, including our entire environment, our functioning consciousnesses and our faculties of perception are all known as impure dependent phenomena. As long as we have grasping and clinging we will experience the impure dependent phenomena. Whatever includes both subject and object are dependent phenomena. We experience things dualistically due to the power of habitual patterns and grasping. Due to ignorance we solidify existing truth. We experience duality because of grasping and clinging even though duality does not truly exist.

Pure Dependent Phenomena

Pure dependent phenomena are the visions and environments of the buddhas and bodhisattvas. Their realization and their understanding are dependent phenomena. As practitioners clear up the duality of subject and object, grasping and clinging onto self and others, we begin to see a new dimension of phenomena that we failed to recognize before. A new dimension of reality gradually arises as we deepen our awareness and strengthen our realization. This is the ultimate state of the Buddha. We will then experience the environment of the buddhas. This is known as the four kayas and the five wisdom displays. We begin to perceive all of this.

According to the Mind Only school, the pure reality that you begin to see when you are a high bodhisattva or a buddha is the original nature. It is the true nature of the mind. When you reveal the true nature of the mind you begin to see what is real. Presently, we are completely covered by the veils and curtains of exaggerations. The curtains of exaggeration shield up all of these phenomenal systems and we don't see them as they are. As we remove the duality curtains we begin to see the true face of the nature of reality as it is because we are inwardly cleansing our mind with our mind. However much you clean your mind determines how much you will begin to experience things in a different way.

The Truly Established Nature

The third category of the Mind Only school is the ultimately existing Final Establishment, Final Fact or Truly Established Nature. The final fact has two sub-divisions. In the Mahayana school everything is pure from the beginning, equally both from the relative level and the absolute level, and from the imputed level and the ultimate level. In a way, everything is equal in the great natural state. Yet when we begin to perceive the true nature, then there are two aspects: subject and object.

The first aspect of the final fact is called the "Unchangeable Final Fact". The Unchangeable Truly Established Nature" is the true nature. It is also called the great emptiness. This appears as the objective aspect of the Truly Established Nature. The second aspect is known as the "Unmistakable Knowledge of the Truly Established Nature". This is the wisdom, knowledge or intelligence that sees the true nature exactly as it is. It is the subjective aspect of the Final Fact. When you discover the unchangeable nature by the unmistakable wisdom of the final fact then you become enlightened and achieve buddhahood.

This is the brief essential meaning of the Mind Only school. The Mind Only school was not started by Vasubandhu. It is not something that the great master Vasubandhu made. Vasubandhu reclarified or rekindled these authentic teachings of Buddha Shakyamuni. Buddha's teachings gradually move deeper, deeper and deeper. That's how Buddha taught. The Mind Only school is a Mahayana teaching. It is an essential teaching of the Buddha. Therefore it is a very special teaching that we should not just leave as a set of ideas. We must put these teachings into practice ourselves and use these techniques to bring full realization of Dzogchen. This is what we really need to do. In order to do this here are some brief instructions on how to meditate according to the Mind Only school.

Meditation Instructions

Just as with all of the practices that we do, we must begin with the beautiful motivation of joy and appreciation. Feel the preciousness of every moment in every aspect of our life. Bring out joy and appreciation from your heart. This is Dharma according to Buddhism. This is not some strange thing that we are trying to add to our Buddhist practices. This very motivation is the practice. It is the Dharma. Therefore bring these qualities more into heart and to mind. We should try to make ourselves familiar with this. Due to our grasping, duality mind, we are always carried away by emotions. These are exaggerations. They are imputed, imaginary phenomena. Instead of being carried by them we should try to bring out, reinforce and return to our true nature of joy and appreciation, and become familiar with this. Even though it is our nature, ego-clinging doesn't let us become familiar with where we actually belong. Therefore try to get used to being joyful and appreciative; grateful to be what we already are. This is necessary and important. Together with this attitude, take refuge and develop bodhichitta.

Once you really have these beautiful thoughts, the main part of the meditation is exactly as it is said in this teaching. Everything—all phenomena; every one of our perceptions; every one of our conceptions; every one of our thoughts—are no other than the mind. No matter what big visions you may have or whatever perceptions or conceptions arise; no matter what size it is, it is only your perception. Your perception is your mind. Your conception is your mind.

Just as we have discussed, and just as the Buddha and master Vasubandhu said so many times, we always follow after our feelings. We are so attached to our feelings. Ideas and feelings are so important to regular sentient beings. We are always stalking them all of the time. Conceptions, ideas, and feelings are so important to us. We are always clinging onto to them. We're struggling with this. But this struggle is really no other than the mind. So whatever comes, recognize that it is mind. When you practice it doesn't mean that you cannot experience anything. When practicing you should let it all dissolve and return to the space of the nature. And relax on your mind.

Master Vasubandhu repeated the Buddha's words so clearly: There is no perception outside that comes to us. We are chasing the perceptions. We are the chasers of perceptions and the chasers of conceptions. We are the chasers of feelings. We are the ones who chase. *They* really don't chase us.

According to the Mind-only school, this means that we are chasing the imputations. We are chasing all kinds of imputed phenomena that don't really exist. We are making ourselves more artificial and more exaggerated as we chase phenomenal existence. For that reason, instead of chasing, look inwardly and relax when you practice. Be relaxed on the natural state. Don't let these exaggerations spoil our nature.

When we relax our mind in the natural state it is free from the two dualities: both subject and object. It is original nature, the state of freshness. That is how we should relax. Just this is original nature; the true nature; the self-awareness nature. It is the real nature. It is not exaggeration. It is not artificial, imputed or labelled. It is really true. So relax in this natural state for as long as you have time or are able to.

When we're meditating of course thoughts will come up. Even if we are not meditating, during our post-meditation thoughts will come up. Feelings will come up. Sensations will come up. All of these experiences will arise due to our habitual patterns. But using the power of mindfulness we should try to restrengthen our awareness that everything is nothing but the mind. It is mind. Occasionally think about this throughout the day. This is particularly important during challenging times. We should not just be carried away by our exaggerations. Instead look inwardly and recognize that this is mind. Even if we are having good times we should also remember that everything is mind. When good feelings come we should see them as mind. When bad feelings come we should also see them as mind. This is really true. We are not just making up more exaggerations of imputed phenomena. Everything is really mind. Therefore bring yourself back to the knowledge that you learned, studied and practiced. Come back. This is known as maintaining the practice or meditation.

Throughout the day bring up more thoughts of love, kindness and compassion for all living beings. Love, compassion and kindness are the authentic nature of the mind. Love, kindness and compassion are the pure dependent nature. Love, kindness and compassion are the pure truly established nature. Therefore bring up these qualities. You should feel great love and compassion for all sentient beings. Most sentient beings are carried by the exaggerations of imputed phenomena. They are struggling with this even though it is not really real. Still they are just struggling. It is like a nightmare—being continually carried by and constantly crushed by these duality fabrications. It is the same for all these beings. And yet all of this started out of nothing. It began with ignorance. For this very reason, feel love, compassion, kindness; more love and stronger compassion. How I can help and support these suffering beings? How I can remove their pain? Think of all of the ways that you can help all beings. How can I reach out to all beings? Have these thoughts throughout the day and then restrengthen your realization and your knowledge.

Finish by doing the dedication prayers as we usually do—with a good heart. This means that these dedications are the sparking qualities of the pure nature. They are the pure dependent nature and pure truly established nature. For these reasons they are very special. Really wish that your practice will help you and others. As we've been discussing, all is mind. When you project the mind in this way it brings tremendous benefits to us and to all beings. Therefore we should also do good dedication and aspiration prayers.

By this practice we will gradually achieve the truly established nature—the unchangeable pure nature. Unmistakable knowledge of the truly established nature will begin to appear by doing these practices. The dawn of this will come.

This is our brief summary of the teachings of the Mind Only school.

Dedication

May the victory banner of the fearless teachings of
the ancient tradition be raised.
May the victorious drum of the teaching and practice of Dharma
resound in the ten directions.
May the lion's roar of reasoning pervade the three places.
May the light of unequalled virtues increase.

May all the temples and monasteries,
All the readings and recitations of the Dharma flourish.
May the sangha always be in harmony,
And may their aspirations be achieved.

At this very moment for the peoples and nations of the earth,
May not even the names disease, famine, war,
and suffering be heard.
But rather may pure conduct, merit, wealth, and
prosperity increase,
And may supreme good fortune and well being always arise.

About the Authors

Khenchen Palden Sherab Rinpoche

Venerable Khenchen Palden Sherab Rinpoche is a renowned scholar and meditation master of Nyingma, the Ancient School of Tibetan Buddhism.

He was born on May 10, 1942 in the Dhoshul region of Kham, Eastern Tibet, near the sacred mountain Jowo Zegyal. On the morning of his birth a small snow fell with the flakes in the shape of lotus petals. Among his ancestors were many great scholars, practitioners, and treasure revealers.

His family was semi-nomadic, living in the village during the winter and moving with the herds to high mountain pastures where they lived in yak hair tents during the summers. The monastery for the Dhoshul region is called Gochen and his father's family had the hereditary responsibility for administration of the business affairs of the monastery. His grandfather had been both administrator and chantmaster in charge of the ritual ceremonies.

He started his education at the age of four at Gochen monastery, which was founded by Tsasum Lingpa. At the age of twelve he entered Riwoche monastery and completed his studies just before the Chinese invasion of Tibet reached that area. His root teacher was the illustrious Khenpo Tenzin Dragpa (Katog Khenpo Akshu).

In 1960, Rinpoche and his family were forced into exile, escaping to India. Eventually in 1967 he was appointed head of the Nyingmapa department of the Central Institute of Higher Tibetan Studies in Sarnath. He held this position for seventeen years, as an abbot, dedicating all his time and energy to ensure the survival and spread of the Buddhist teachings.

Rinpoche moved to the United States in 1984 to work closely with H.H. Dudjom Rinpoche, the supreme head of the Nyingmapa lineage. In 1985, Venerable Khenchen Palden Sherab Rinpoche and his brother Venerable Khenpo Tsewang Dongyal Rinpoche founded the Dharma Samudra Publishing Company. In 1988, they founded the Padmasambhava Buddhist Center, which has centers throughout the United States, as well as in Puerto Rico, Russia and India. The primary center is Padma Samye Ling, located in Delaware County, New York. Padmasambhava Buddhist Center also includes a traditional Tibetan Buddhist monastery and nunnery at the holy site of Deer Park in Sarnath, India.

Rinpoche travels extensively within the United States and throughout the world, giving teachings and empowerments at numerous retreats and seminars, in addition to establishing meditation centers.

His three volumes of collected works in Tibetan include:

Opening the Eyes of Wisdom, a commentary on Sangye Yeshe's *Lamp of the Eye of Contemplation*;

Waves of the Ocean of Devotion, a biography-praise to Nubchen Sangye Yeshe, and *Vajra Rosary*, biographies of his main incarnations;

The Mirror of Mindfulness, an explanation of the six bardos;

Advice from the Ancestral Vidyadhara, a commentary on Padmasambhava's *Stages of the Path, Heap of Jewels*;

Blazing Clouds of Wisdom and Compassion, a commentary on the hundred-syllable mantra of Vajrasattva;

The Ornament of Vairochana's Intention, a commentary on the *Heart Sutra*;

Opening the Door of Blessings, a biography of Machig Labdron;

Lotus Necklace of Devotion, a biography of Khenchen Tenzin Dragpa;

The Essence of Diamond Clear Light, an outline and structural

analysis of *The Aspiration Prayer of Samantabhadra*;
The Lamp of Blazing Sun and Moon, a commentary on Mipham's *Wisdom Sword*;
The Ornament of Stars at Dawn, an outline and structural analysis of Vasubandhu's *Twenty Verses*;
Pleasure Lake of Nagarjuna's Intention, general summary of Madhyamaka;
Supreme Clear Mirror, an introduction to Buddhist logic;
White Lotus, an explanation of prayers to Guru Rinpoche;
Smiling Red Lotus, short commentary on the prayer to Yeshe Tsogyal;
Clouds of Blessings; an explanation of prayers to Terchen Tsasum Lingpa; and other learned works, poems, prayers and sadhanas.

Khenpo Tsewang Dongyal Rinpoche

Venerable Khenpo Tsewang Dongyal Rinpoche was born in the Dhoshul region of Kham in eastern Tibet on June 10, 1950. On that summer day in the family tent, Rinpoche's birth caused his mother no pain. The next day, his mother Pema Lhadze moved the bed where she had given birth. Beneath it she found growing a beautiful and fragrant flower which she plucked and offered to Chenrezig on the family altar.

Soon after his birth three head lamas from Jadchag monastery came to his home and recognized him as the reincarnation of Khenpo Sherab Khyentse. Khenpo Sherab Khyentse, who had been the former head abbot lama at Gochen monastery, was a renowned scholar and practitioner who spent much of his life in retreat.

Rinpoche's first Dharma teacher was his father, Lama Chimed Namgyal Rinpoche. Beginning his schooling at the age of five, he entered Gochen monastery. His studies were interrupted by the Chinese invasion and his family's escape to India. In India his father and brother continued his education until he entered the Nyingmapa Monastic School of northern India, where he studied until 1967. He then entered the Central Institute of Higher Tibetan Studies, which was then a part of Sanskrit University in Varanasi, where he received his B.A. degree in 1975. He also attended Nyingmapa University in West Bengal, where he received another B.A. and an M.A. in 1977.

In 1978, Rinpoche was enthroned as the abbot of the Wish-fulfilling Nyingmapa Institute in Boudanath, Nepal by H.H. Dudjom Rinpoche, and later became the abbot of the Department of Dharma Studies, where he taught poetry, grammar, philosophy and psychology. In 1981, H.H. Dudjom Rinpoche appointed Rinpoche as the abbot of the Dorje

Nyingpo center in Paris, France. In 1982 he was asked to work with H.H. Dudjom Rinpoche at the Yeshe Nyingpo center in New York. During the 1980's, until H.H. Dudjom Rinpoche's mahaparinirvana in 1987, Rinpoche continued working closely with H.H. Dudjom Rinpoche, often traveling with him as his translator and attendant.

In 1988, Rinpoche and his brother founded the Padmasambhava Buddhist Center. Since that time he has served as a spiritual director at the various Padmasambhava centers throughout the world. He maintains an active traveling and teaching schedule with his brother Khenchen Palden Sherab Rinpoche.

Khenpo Tsewang Rinpoche has authored two books of poetry on the life of Guru Rinpoche, including *Praise to the Lotus Born: A Verse Garland of Waves of Devotion*, and a unique two-volume cultural and religious history of Tibet entitled *The Six Sublime Pillars of the Nyingma School*, which details the historical bases of the Dharma in Tibet from the sixth through ninth centuries. At present, this is one of the only books yet written that conveys the dharma activities of this historical period in such depth. Khenpo Rinpoche has also co-authored a number of books in English on Dharma subjects with his brother Khenchen Palden Sherab Rinpoche, including *Ceaseless Echoes of the Great Silence: A Commentary on the Heart Sutra*; *Prajnaparamita: The Six Perfections*; *Door to Inconceivable Wisdom and Compassion*; *Lion's Gaze: A Commentary on the Tsig Sum Nedek*; and *Opening Our Primordial Nature.*

Other Publications by the Authors

Ceaseless Echoes of the Great Silence:
A Commentary on the Heart Sutra

Prajnaparamita: The Six Perfections

Light of the Three Jewels

Lion's Gaze: A Commentary on the Tsig Sum Nedek

Door to Inconceivable Wisdom and Compassion

Praise to the Lotus Born: A Verse Garland of Waves of Devotion

The Smile of Sun and Moon

Opening to Our Primordial Nature

Opening the Clear Vision of the Vaibhashika and Sautrantika Schools

Opening the Wisdom Door of the Madhyamaka School

Opening the Wisdom Door of the Rangtong and Shentong Views:
A Brief Explanation of the One Taste of the Second
and Third Turnings of the Wheel of Dharma

~

More information about these and other works by
the Venerable Khenpo Rinpoches can be found online at:
www.padmasambhava.org/chiso.

CPSIA information can be obtained
at www.ICGtesting.com
Printed in the USA
FSHW010224020620
70454FS

9 780965 933957